Middle Age Renaissance

Middle Age Renaissance

Body, Mind, and Spirit

DOUG BROOKS

iUniverse, Inc.
Bloomington

Middle Age Renaissance
Body, Mind, and Spirit

iUniverse books may be ordered through booksellers or by contacting:

iUniverse
1663 Liberty Drive
Bloomington, IN 47403
www.iuniverse.com
1-800-Authors (1-800-288-4677)

ISBN: 978-1-4759-6048-8 (sc)
ISBN: 978-1-4759-6046-4 (hc)
ISBN: 978-1-4759-6047-1 (e)

Library of Congress Control Number: 2012920909

Printed in the United States of America

iUniverse rev. date: 11/16/2012

For Douglas, Bryan and ErinLeigh

Thanks to Martin Naparsteck,
a Good friend and writer

Also By Doug Brooks

A Practical Approach to Professional Writing

&

Front Street and Other Poems

DISCLAIMER

The information in this book is for illustrative purposes. The author professes no expertise or authority, just experience. One of the things to consider is that you can change your life without having to establish professional credentials first. I did it, so can you. A doctor should be consulted prior to beginning any exercise routine. And for those readers who find mistakes, questionable information, know that I only wanted to include something for everyone.

Since the completion of this book, life has happened. There have been joys and sorrows, deaths and births. So, please forgive me for any small contradictions in numbers and chronology. I continue to practice what I preach, and endeavor to make sense out of life by wondering, questioning and learning.

CONTENTS

INTRODUCTION

Life moves fast. What does it really mean to be middle age? Does it mean our youth is gone? Does it mean there's more behind us than in front of us? Or does it mean and call for a new beginning? I think it presents an opportunity for a new beginning, a renewal of the body, mind and spirit.

Maybe we're in our thirties, or forties, fifties and we've become complacent. Hell, sitting on the couch drinking beer or iced tea and watching TV or surfing the internet is about all we can muster the energy for after a hard day at work. She's on the phone, the kids are doing whatever they do at the ages they are, and you feel like you're just going through the motions with no direction or goals other than avoiding getting yelled at by someone. So now you're fat, or husky, and out of shape, and don't care. You think you don't care. You do. You do.

You can change your life if you want to. Sure, you've heard that a hundred times before. Your dreams didn't turn out the way you thought they would and you're close to giving up and just settling for the way things are. It doesn't have to be that way. You can change; you can become who you would have become, who you should have become. You're in charge. Just be still a moment and know. It's in you to know. You have to give yourself the opportunity to discover and move forward. You only get one chance as far as I know, and now is your chance to become who you might have become if life had not gotten in the way.

Life gets in the way a lot. We lose jobs, we get divorced, we lose whatever we had we thought we would have forever. We all risk losing everything every day of our lives. Nothing is guaranteed except death. Why not make the most of it all before the inevitable? No one can do it for you except you. You have the power within you to change your life.

Renewing is not just a matter of making your life better; it takes into account those around us who care and want the best. Renewing your body, mind and spirit is all about second chances; and we all deserve second chances. Project ten or fifteen years into the future and ask yourself what you think you might be regretting at that point. And now you have the opportunity to avoid some regrets and find yourself in your future renewed, and the person you always knew you should and could be. Give it a shot; what the hell have you got to lose?

CHAPTER 1

How I Got Started

When someone comments positively on my physique, not that it happens that often, I am sincerely flattered, but humble about it. I usually say thank you and something to the effect, "I have the body of a nineteen year old and he wants it back because I'm getting it all wrinkled." It hasn't always been that way. There were more than a few periods in my life when I was anything but happy with the way I looked physically.

I can still remember as an adolescent being overweight, and totally uncomfortable with how it felt. It was precisely at the time in a young man's life when girls start to become an issue. And there I was, overweight and lacking in confidence. I would fantasize about girls telling me they still liked me even if I was a bit chubby. In fact, some of the girls in my fantasies even preferred me "husky."

Husky. What a word. It's a word to describe overweight boys without being too cruel or obvious. My Mother would take me shopping for clothes in the husky department and I hated every minute of it. Sure, I hated the shopping part in general, but I hated having to shop in the husky department even more. I hated the way my fat spilled out over the tops of my pants when I tried them on. I hated how they seemed to restrict everything, even my confidence. My Mother always commented on how well the pants fit even though they were about six inches too long in order to accommodate my waist. I wanted to wear the ratty old pants that were finally broken in, contoured to my body but too crappy looking to be presentable. I had to sneak out of the house if I wanted to wear my comfortable pants. I even hated walking by mirrors in a department store because of the truth the reflection offered. It wasn't fun, and I just wanted to get something to eat and go home.

I don't think I correlated eating with my weight at that age. It didn't seem America was as overweight in the early sixties as it is now. There was little if any information for adolescents to consult for all of the angst we were feeling about all kinds of things. We were raised by parents who had weathered the Depression, so we were constantly required to be grateful for all kinds of things, including the food we ate. We were always told how lucky we were; no matter what we had we were lucky to have it. Our parents never had anything we had: clothes, food, books, TV, toys, a short walk to school, and everything else that was supposed to make our lives so complete and wonderful. I often wondered how our parents survived at all. I could picture my Mother digging in the dirt for grubs in the thirties just for strength. When my Mother gave me a hard time for complaining and told me to count my blessings. I never came up with a very long list.

There were a lot of things I remember that didn't seem particularly like blessings. I hated the teachers at school making me feel stupid and worthless. When I came home and told my Mother that Sister Lady of Bleeding Gums doubled up her chubby little fist and sent me flying down the hall, she told me I probably deserved it. When I showed her my bloody knuckles from the trumpet teacher hitting me with a steel edged ruler when I hit the wrong valve, she commented on how much my playing had improved. I hated having to adjust the vertical and horizontal hold on the television. I hated having to wear a yellow rubber rain coat in the rain, and those dumb black boots with the buckles. I hated having to wear a hat with ear flaps. Sure we didn't have to stand in line for food, or use ration cards for gas and stuff but we did have to carry out ash cans and be nice to old people and consider all adults, even the stupid ones, as superior. It wasn't easy, and my love life was suffering because of my weight.

One of my first loves was Mrs. Mason, my ninth grade English teacher, and boy was I crazy about her. This was in the mid-sixties, and Mrs. Mason was one of the first hippies I encountered. She wore her hair long, always tied back with sort of a rippling quality to it. She always smelled so good. When she stopped at my desk to help me solve a problem- I had a lot of them - I would almost get dizzy taking in all of her wonderful scents. She smiled and walked really good. I especially liked to watch her walk away. I had even convinced myself that if I wasn't husky she would probably have fallen in love with me. I think the only thing that I learned that year was that I was in love with an older woman who would never notice me because I was fat.

I would even envy my thin friends for the way their clothes fit and how all of the girls seemed to give them more attention than me. I almost felt like a non-person at times. I struggled with my weight for the next three years; high school can be a miserable experience for a lot of reasons. My wardrobe was limited throughout high school; we didn't have a lot of money and I guess my mom thought that I was pretty much on my own when it came to those kind of things after the age of thirteen. I mean, I had a job through high school .

I bought a car and paid my own insurance and took care of my basic needs, which consisted of paying for gas for my car, eating as much fast, crappy food as I could, and trying to figure out how to find somebody who was old enough to buy me and my friends beer for the weekend. So, like a lot of young men my age growing up in the sixties, I was pretty much on my own when it came to trying to figure out who

I was and whether or not I had any value. It wasn't long before the government, through the draft, let us know what our value really was. But that is just one of the many things we baby boomers struggled with as far as our identity was concerned. Who I was eventually bolstered in my senior year of high school when a young woman came along who really liked me for who I was, not how much my tummy didn't spill over the top of my jeans. I finally had a true girlfriend - such a neat idea. "I have a girlfriend - oh, my girlfriend and I - it's my girlfriend on the phone." Having someone really care about you does help, but more importantly, having someone to care about is even better. But I was still the husky guy, or as my friends would occasionally say, "fat boy." I didn't like that, although I would laugh along with them when they said it. I was too embarrassed not to. We did or didn't do a lot of things because we were too embarrassed. Hey, I didn't want to come across as wimpy and unmanly. Looking back, I think, why the hell did I give a shit? But I did and I was fat.

I graduated from high school in 1971 and was grateful I did. I spent the summer after high school being basically inert. I drank a lot of beer, ate a lot of fast food, sat around doing nothing constructive and gaining weight. By the end of the summer I had reached my heaviest weight ever and looked it. I still had the same girlfriend and she seemed to care about me no matter what I weighed, but I was still unhappy. Hell, I had the fat gene. There wasn't a bony person in my family. In fact, I think my family's philosophy was, the bigger the better, the fatter the healthier. So I came by my weight, as my Mother would say, honestly. By the time Fall of 1971 came along, I was up to almost 190 pounds at 5 foot nine inches. It might not sound too terribly bad, but it was mainly fat; there wasn't a hell of a lot of muscle there. I looked fat and felt fat. I was pretty much down to one pair of pants that fit. Now when I look at the pictures taken of my girlfriend and me, I wonder where she is. She practically disappears in my presence. What to do?

I did try exercising a bit at this point in my life. My Godfather had given me a set of weights when I was younger and I had never used them in the past. When I think about it now, maybe he was trying to help me then. He might have been; he was a good guy. So, I spent a couple of days lifting these weights this way and that with no results, so I quit. Hell, I figured, how long should it take? If I wasn't beefed up after a week, what was the point? It was about this time that the draft lottery was drawn. Remember that war we had going on, that it was the responsibility of America's teenagers to win? The war in Vietnam wasn't new but it also wasn't over; go figure. I drew a low number. My chances of being drafted were pretty good. My friends and I sat in a friend's living room drinking beer and bourbon drowning our sorrows or toasting our good luck, depending on what your number was, and my life changed. I decided to get a jump on it. So without talking to anyone, I went down to the draft board and "joined the draft." Joining the draft ensured I would only have to do two years. That's really all the government wanted from most of us anyway. It really didn't make any difference; it was just like being drafted. At least this way I had some control over my life; it was my choice. Well, maybe not really; that and putting our lives on the line for their agenda. So now I only had about a week to live out the sedentary life I had fashioned for myself. I only had one more week to eat and drink and be lazy and apathetic. I wish I would have known that the army wouldn't have any patience with me and my fat, out of shape body.

Basic training was anything but easy for me. I took Basic at Fort Dix in New Jersey. I always thought you needed a passport to go to New Jersey, but I found out that I was wrong. I was overweight and out of shape. More than anything else, I remember when the drill sergeants started to make us run everyplace that we went. I was always at the end of the group, behind everyone else, with the other overweight, out of shape recruits. I was only nineteen years old but physically inadequate for the simple task of running more than a few yards. It was tough; it was a struggle. One thing I can say is that the army knows its stuff. After two months I was not only keeping up with the rest of the recruits, but I had also lost almost forty pounds. I lost it even eating three meals a day and snacking and drinking the occasional beer. But I was active; I had to be active; I was forced to be active. But once training ended, I went back to my old ways.

Once I was sent overseas I was limited to whatever duties the army determined I was responsible for; my activity declined. And like any good enlisted man, I figured out ways to get out of as much duty as I could. I didn't get back up to my heaviest weight, but I did regain some weight. Of course the army tried to provide us with various activities that should have kept us in shape in addition to our regular duties, which were strenuous enough. We played organized volleyball, softball and even amateur boxing. Unfortunately we were only required to expend as much energy as we wanted. Our duties did keep us moving here, there and everywhere, but it was mostly cardio kind of stuff: we humped through our duties. After my two years, the army and I agreed that we had enough of each other and I was discharged. I went home to the loving warmth of my family, my worthless friends and unemployment. During the war in Vietnam, discharged soldiers were eligible for unemployment benefits, and I took full advantage of what I considered free money. I rented my own apartment, signed for my check once a week and had what I considered was a well deserved good time; I also gained more weight. The sweet life can't last forever, so I decided to enroll in college; hell, I had the GI bill coming to me. Once again, I had the opportunity to get some cash and only have to go to school to collect it. I went to school, partied and gained more weight. During this period of self discovery, I became engaged to the young woman who had waited for me to come home. We planned our wedding and I continued to act like a twenty-one-year-old without direction or responsibility.

During this very confusing period of my life, I drank too much, got into too many bar fights, ate too much bad food, experimented a lot with too many drugs and considered myself immortal. I was losing control of where I was going and losing sight of who I was. I got married, continued going to school, worked in the summers and ate even more bad food, and drank even more than I should have. I guess my wife had a lot of patience and didn't care that I was once again an overweight slob. Years later I discovered that it wasn't patience that she had for me; she just didn't know what to do. Revelation: she was young, too. So, over the course of the first year of our marriage I gained the prescribed amount of weight newlyweds are supposed to gain on top of the fat I was already carrying. But then something happened; something that changed my life, not for the better, just changed it.

I woke up one morning and started to get dressed and realized that my pants didn't fit; I was devastated. I couldn't see my dick when I took a piss, and my thighs spread out like two sides of beef waiting for the butcher. I changed. I started watching what I ate. I ate carrots at night for a snack. I started doing sit-ups and pushups and curling the living room stool in my efforts to try and make a difference. It worked. Within a few short months I had dropped about twenty pounds and finally looked good for the first time since Basic.

I kept this routine up for years after my rebirth. I exercised almost every day after work. I worked out through the births of my children, through job changes, through various college experiences. I did eventually complete three college degrees including a Master's in English. I became obsessive about the weight thing.

I watched my caloric intake like a banker watches the clock. I would ask my wife, my Mother, "is this fattening?" as I put something into my mouth. And, of course, they would always say no. I got to the point over the years where I would only eat one meal a day because I was so worried about gaining weight. I even began to take laxatives so I would never feel like I was full, because feeling full meant getting fat, to my way of thinking. I hated anything tight around my waist; I slit the elastic on my underwear so I wouldn't be aware of the confinement. I kept most of this obsessive behavior to myself; it was something I could control. This went on for almost fifteen years; and it wasn't easy. I looked good, like I was in shape, but I wasn't. My nutrition was terrible and I looked way too thin. The lowest point of this stage of my life came when I contracted a lung infection and my weight dropped down to under 130 pounds. This weight didn't look good on my 5 foot 9 inch frame; I looked like death in the rain. Something had to change.

The change in my life came from an unlikely source. My wife and I separated and I moved out and was truly on my own for the first time in a very long time. I didn't really put on any weight because I never went to the store and ended up eating a lot of whatever was around, like soup and stuff, but I was still out of shape. The unlikely source that helped to turn my life around, at least physically, was my oldest son. It was at this time when he started high school and decided that he wanted to play lacrosse. Someone suggested to him that he start working out at a gym to get in shape for the demands of the sport. So he joined a gym and needed a ride there every day after school.

I was a year away from turning forty and feeling all of those things that go along with that milestone. I felt pretty good about the way I looked, but deep down I knew I was in just as poor shape as I was when I was fat, maybe worse. I had a fairly decent job: college professor teaching English at Monroe Community College in Rochester, New York. It was a good job, but didn't offer a lot of opportunity for physical activity. I continued to exercise at home, but it was boring and I still watched what I ate a little bit too closely. A change seemed in order.

One day my son got out of school early and went straight to the gym with his friends. I was to pick him up there and give him a ride home. When I pulled into the gym parking lot I noticed these behemoths coming and going. I mean, some of these guys were really huge. You know when you see guys like that out on the street you wonder where they come from; well, now I knew; they come from gyms like this. There had to be a correlation...smart, right? I went up to the second floor of the gym and stopped at the reception desk because you had to go through a turnstile to get in. Coincidentally a former student of mine was manning the front desk. We got to talking about a variety of things including membership prices. The price sounded reasonable, and he even walked me into the gym to show me the facilities. All I could see were a lot of foreign looking machines and weights and bar bells and dumb bells and the people lifting them. They weren't all beefy guys busting out of their clothes; many were just normal looking people working out and seemingly having a good time. My son noticed me and we left. He was just beginning to get at the age where he wasn't embarrassed to be seen with me, but not quite. The next day I joined the gym. I decided to pay on a monthly basis; I figured why commit myself before I really know what I'm doing.

MOTIVATION

Why at this point in my life, almost forty years old, did I finally find the motivation, the incentive to begin and stick with a workout routine? I think one of the primary stumbling blocks people have to sticking with a routine is commitment. Sure, it's easy to start one; hell, I see people come and go at the gym like it's a bus station. They become familiar faces for a few weeks, then they are rarely seen again. One of the reasons people who go to a gym on a regular basis make friends is that the majority of the people who they run into are the ones who go all the time; you just see the same people. More often than not you don't even know their names, just the faces. So why do I, why do they, keep going day in and day out? There are probably just as many reasons as there are people who go regularly. But I do believe there are probably some common reasons committed work out people share.

One of the most popular excuses people have for not exercising on a regular basis is not having enough time to commit to it. Well, yeah, we all have busy lives, but I think there are few things as important as our health, and self-image. Most of us have plenty of time to sit in front of the television and relax and unwind, or whatever rationalization we might come up with. Yes, we do need time to relax and not think, but how much is the real issue. Hey, I sit in front of the idiot box just like everyone else and let my brain atrophy every night. But I also have already worked out for the day. I really think it comes down to saving up time for something or other. What the hell are we saving up time for? What are we going to use this saved up time to do? Everything we do today seems to revolve around the acquisition of more time. But, to do what?

As a teacher I see this manifest itself quite often. Students always seem to have time issues. It relates to when they come to class, when they are late for class, when they have to leave early from class and the degree they are rushing to be finished with their education. They are in a hurry. But in a hurry for what? I suppose some people are really into this completion thing. There are occasions in the classroom when I have students working either in groups or independently. Invariably someone will ask, "Can we leave when we're finished?" They are always in a hurry. A number of years ago I gave this question some serious thought. I would ask the students why they wanted to leave early. They always had a whole bunch of neat reasons. They had a doctor's appointment, (somehow I avoid making such appointments during class hours), they have to give someone a ride, they are hungry, they have to study for something else (this pisses me off), they're tired, and on and on. So, I started offering them an option. Yes, they could leave early but they had to write me a 250 word essay explaining what they did with the extra time that was so important to them. Often the time issue was just a matter of minutes. Very few students have taken me up on this compromise. And the few who did ended up writing essays detailing how they sat outside of the classroom and waited, or went to their next class early, basically just wasted the time. It's not that they really needed the extra time; we have just been programmed to collect all of the extra minutes we can for some future use.

The time issue is not only a phenomena for students. We all are collectors of extra time; we're all in a hurry to get it done, complete things, finish up what we have started as quickly as possible. I mean, just sit in any break room or cafeteria in any organization in this country, and pay attention to some of the conversations taking place. Sure, we hear people bitching and complaining about their jobs and all that goes along with that. What a way to spend eight hours of every day. I digress. But we also hear people talking about retirement. People share that issue; someday everyone is going to retire. They talk about benefits, IRA's, 401K's, investments, how much they will have available when that fateful day comes along. They talk about the years remaining until they can finally relax and take it easy, and have the time they want to do whatever they were saving up to do most of their lives. Again, why the hurry?

I mean, if we spend thirty or forty years of our lives looking forward to retirement, what's left? What do we look forward to after that: Death? The only time we really have available to us, the only time we can count on, believe in and make the most of is the Moment. The past is gone and the future is uncertain. No matter how much we think we can control tomorrow, it always remains uncertain. Therefore why don't we just slow down a bit and reestablish our priorities.

When you really think about it, the only thing we have control over is ourselves; and even that can be an issue. Many, not all, people spend a good portion of their lives working too much to make extra money to buy a bunch of crap they never really needed and to impress people who they don't like anyway. We are so tied up into our careers that we don't even see our kids grow up. One minute we're changing diapers and the next we're applauding at their college graduations: we blinked. I fell into that attitude during a good portion of my unhealthy life. Every Monday morning as I reluctantly went into work I was wishing it was Friday. I was wishing five days out of every seven away. And when the weekend did come, I generally wasted the time anyway because I was getting ready for Monday morning again. I was trying to do all of my living in two days. I was drinking seven days worth of beer in two days, I was eating seven days worth of bad food in two days, I was trying to get seven days worth of recreation and entertainment into two days. So by Monday morning I felt like crap, but I couldn't wait for Friday to do it all over again. What's up with that?

Let's say we all live a long, productive life. And there we are: 94 years old and finally we are about to pass on to the next world. Die. As our final moments approach do we request that all of the possessions we acquired over our lifetime be brought to our bedside? Do we demand that our bank statements be placed upon our chests to heave with our final breaths? Do we request we be propped up by the window so our final image is that fancy car we so loved to drive? No. All that will really matter is the investment we made in ourselves and the people we love, the people who love us. That's what matters and we all know it. But do we know it with a big K, or a small k? So at this point one might be asking what does all of this have to do with working out, with exercising? Believe it or not, it has quite a bit to do with how we feel physically. Be patient; we'll get to the benefits after we finish addressing this time issue.

So where can we find the time to work out? It's there; each day has twenty four hours to choose from. Look at your day's schedules and ask yourself how much of the day is wasted; we need to be honest here. How much time do you need to work out? That all depends on what you want to achieve. I have found that thirty minutes a day is the minimum amount of time you should devote, forty minutes is better, fifty is great, an hour is ideal. You figure it out; but suffice it to say, I bet the time is there, you just have to find it. Do it in the morning before work. Go on you lunch hour. I go various times during the day for a number of reasons. My schedule as a college teacher is always in flux. When I do go during the lunch hours, I do see many people in the gym who have taken their lunch breaks to work out. It might be a bit of a rush, but it is worth it. They eat their lunch in the car before, or after, preferably after. There are showers in the gym if you are prone to sweating and smelling after a workout. Bring a towel. Or go after work.

I have found that the ideal time for me to work out is after work before I go home. I have learned that if I go home first the chances of me going to the gym are limited. I incorporate my after work exercise routine right into my daily schedule. It acts like a buffer between work and home. Do I feel like going to the gym every day after work? Do I dream about pushing around heavy weights for forty five minutes all day with anticipation? Hell no. More often that not, I don't even feel like going after work; all I want to do is go home and turn on the television and sit on the couch and eat Cheetos. But I don't.

I have discovered that the hardest part of going to the gym almost every day is not the workout; it's the getting there. The distance between work and the gym is where the danger is. I am fortunate in that I am only five or so minutes away from the gym I go to, but it's not the distance that presents the problem: it's the attitude we have on the way. It is a matter of direction, not making the turn for home, but making the turn for the gym. Success comes everyday when I pull into the parking lot and shut my car off. I am there and I am there for a reason. I feel better walking into the gym. I feel even better heading for the locker room knowing I have once again made the right decision. Once I'm changed and begin my workout, the apprehension I felt between work and the gym is gone. I am glad I am there; I always feel better after a workout. I have discovered that when you least feel like going is when you most should. Find the time; it is there.

But time isn't always the biggest factor that keeps some people from getting in shape during their middle years. What's the primary difference between me and the overweight, middle aged guy who can only see his dick in a mirror? I am committed to a workout routine: that's it. It's a mind set; it's a change of attitude; it's a desire to be all I can be, at least physically. And the really good news is, it is Never too late. Remember that husky kid in the mirror of the department store: well now he's a fat, or just out of shape, middle aged man who knows he should be exercising, but doesn't. Why not? What are you waiting for? No one can do it for you; you and only you can do it. The benefits are there to be discovered. There is a similar issue I often bring up with my students when we discuss liking what you do as opposed to how much money you make. I tell them, liking what you do, not wishing it was Friday on Monday morning, is far and away more important than how much money you make; I tell them they will discover that money will become secondary in their lives if they are lucky. But they have to discover that themselves; no matter how much I try to convince them, they have to discover that on their own. It's the same with working out; it has to be discovered by each person. But if you don't try, you'll never know the benefits involved.

BENEFITS

Once you begin a workout program something has to motivate you to keep at it day in and day out. What kept me at it, and still does after more than 20 years, were the benefits I began to notice even after only three weeks. Most people who join a gym usually don't last three weeks; two weeks seems to be the extent for most people. If they would just wait that extra week, I believe they would keep at it. The primary difference I noticed after only three weeks is that I felt better; I just felt better physically and emotionally. And isn't that something we are all searching for, just to feel better? I mean, our lives are loaded with all kinds of stresses. We get all bummed out about work, our social lives, family challenges, traffic in the morning, weather, an out of order coffee machine, stupid people, asshole bosses, and alarm clocks. So what do we do when stress gets us by the short hairs? We drink, we take medication, we drink, we go to therapy, we drink, we buy self help books, and we drink as we try to cope with life. Well, wake the hell up: it's life. What the hell did we expect? It ain't like TV, so shut the damn thing off and start working out. Stress is part of life and unless we shut ourselves away in a closet (although personally I find that locking myself in a closet for two or three weeks at a time does effectively relieve me of stress) life will go on and not always meet our needs; life will sometimes be difficult; life will sometimes give us stress. I always think when I am on my way to the gym and not wanting to go how much better I always feel during and after a work out. It's almost like I just woke up after a decent night's sleep, had a cup of coffee, and took a decent dump even before my day really got started. It is often like a mid-day renewal.

I think a lot of it has to do with releasing pheromones when muscles are challenged and pushed. When muscles are challenged to break down and rebuild, it stimulates the brain to release those chemicals that give us that feeling of well being. I sometimes walk into the gym with my ass dragging on the ground, but always walk out with more energy and a sense of accomplishment. It's like my Mom used to say, "It's good for what ails you." The physical benefits are certainly there, but I really believe the emotional benefits are the reasons I continue to go and will continue to workout as long as I can, which means as long as I am alive.

Well, I might not really have the body of a nineteen year old, but I certainly don't have the body of the typical middle aged man in his late forties. Recently I went to the doctor's for a routine examination. I was weighed and poked and prodded and stuck and subjected to all the stuff that goes along with an exam. I commented to the doctor that according to the weight chart I was obese. At five foot nine and one hundred and sixty five pounds, I was at least ten pounds over my limit. He told me that the chart didn't take into account muscle weight as opposed to fat weight. When I was checked for fat content, the results were that my weight consisted of only 13% body fat; which is excellent for anyone of any age. He also went on to comment when I expressed my concerns about my weight that I didn't have the body of someone my age...I was in excellent physical shape.

Being in good shape at my age means a lot of things to me. It means I still wear the same size pants I wore as a teenager, before I got really heavy. I don't even try pants on when I go shopping; although I don't do that very often because I truly hate shopping. I would rather bathe pit bulls than shop. I just buy them off the rack: size 32 waist and I am almost 60. The length depends on how tall I fell on that particular day. Being in good shape also means I have the energy to do what I need, want to do during the day. Just recently the English Department played the Business Department in softball; we're always playing them in something and I think they usually cheat. But they didn't cheat in the softball game because we had an umpire and beat them 8 to 1. I enjoyed the game very much, not only because we finally beat them at something, but because I was physically up to the challenge. I hit, I ran, I fielded and didn't have to sit in a hot tub after because I was sore.

The key to getting in shape in middle age is the motivation to continue to go once started. Even if you already have a workout routine that you follow on a regular basis this book may offer some additional information that might just help you adjust your routine, might help you try some new things that you haven't considered, and might lead you into more positive directions to make the middle years and the years beyond healthy and more enjoyable. Turning into a slob is a choice, not an inevitability. I believe most people choose to be lazy, and put off things like working out. It's time to look good and feel good: it's never too late.

CHAPTER 2

CHOICES AND DECISIONS

WHY CHOOSE A GYM

With the initial idea of wanting to spend a little more time with my son, the original gym I joined was the one he joined. He joined because it was close to his school and that's where his friends went: certainly not uncommon reasons for a teenager to make a choice. Another reason I followed him was this particular gym only required members pay on a monthly basis. I found this option attractive because I wasn't sure how long I would stay with it and I didn't want to commit to some kind of long term thing. But there are benefits to long term commitment: more on that later. So I paid my thirty dollars for the first month's membership and I was good to go.

The day came when I was once again to pick up my son and some of his friends from school and drop them at the gym. But instead of just dropping them off, I went into my trunk, retrieved my bag and went in with them. My son, to say the least, was somewhat surprised. I assured him I would pretend I didn't know him and cramp his style. He was at the age where he wanted people to think he had no parents, that he was most probably raised by wolves. My plan was to basically duplicate the rudimentary workout I occasionally practiced at home and to take it from there. It wasn't long before I realized I might be out of place at this particular gym.

One thing I have discovered over the past 20 years is that there are very different types of gyms: it all depends on what you want to accomplish and how you want to do it. This particular gym was what I refer to as the "testosterone" type. It had all of the best types of equipment. It had the machines for working every possible muscle of the body and then some; it had more free weights and bars and benches than one could desire. It had mirrors in all of the right places to view technique and progress or to just watch other people. It even boasted a juice bar right inside the gym proper. But more than anything else, it had plenty. of large men with big muscles and angry looks on their faces. It even had more than a few women with big muscles and angry looks on their faces. Noises too: the gym was a symphony of grunting and clanging and encouraging words of advice from workout partners. It was an environment I was unfamiliar with. These people looked more than serious about what they were doing.

I mean, one doesn't often see such physical specimens in their daily lives. These guys looked like they were out of Masters of the Universe. They had muscles on top of muscles. Why don't we see these guys just walking down the street, or eating at McDonald's, or shopping, or working next to us on the job? Well, I finally figured out that we don't see these guys because they are always in the gym. I mean, looking the way they do must take lots and lots of work and other things as well.

When I started to frequent this gym, I often wondered why two or three of these guys would be huddled in one of the bathroom stalls. I wasn't about to ask for fear of being initiated into some weird gym cult. It wasn't until my son explained to me that I finally understood. Kids today know so much more than we did at their age. He told me they were either buying, selling, or administering steroids. Made sense to me. I don't think God intended people to get that big without a little help from the world of chemistry. Hey, I didn't judge, I only observed. But I of course had to have yet another obligatory discussion with my son about the evils of steroid use. Before I could I had to do some research because I had no idea what the evils of steroid use were. Thankfully I did discover there were plenty of evils associated with the abuse of steroids. What really caught his attention was the shrinkage of testicles associated with the use of steroids. There aren't a lot of teen age boys who are willing to risk that. By the way, we're talking anabolic steroids here. That's all you really need to know: just stay away from them. Doing it the natural way is much healthier and satisfying, especially for we in the middle years of our lives. Last thing we need is anything else on our bodies shrinking.

You know how when you join something new that making friends, people to say hello to, is important to the overall experience. Hell, it can be in a club, bowling league, church group, book club, cult or whatever. Knowing others who share the same interest is part of what makes the association satisfying. What I discovered at this particular gym is that most of the members had little need for more people to say hello to. They were too busy making noise and getting bigger. And don't forget, I was supposed to pretend I didn't know my son even though he got in and out of my car with me. So I was more or less on my own, an island among mountains. I did renew my membership for another month, and another and another. I think I was holding out hope that my son would discover that this gym thing would be a good bonding experience for the both of us, but it was not to be. After six months I accepted the fact that I was out of place in this gym; a worm among eagles, a flea among dogs. I suppose my kind of passive attitude about working out clashed with their aggressive attitude. That revelation on my part might have had something to do with the fact that on more than one occasion a behemoth bumped into me, knocking me into lockers, machines, the floor. Once could have been an accident, but not at least once a week. Were they sending me a message; was I being paranoid; did they really dislike me? I don't know, but I did figure it was time to search for alternatives. I wasn't discouraged; I had invested six months into this endeavor and felt better and looked better and wasn't about to give it up. I was hooked, but not crazy. Besides, one of my son's friends had gotten his driver's license; so my services were no longer required.

The next gym I joined was far better that the first; it was more conducive to what I wanted to accomplish and the environment I wanted to accomplish it in. It's like lots of other things: you have to do a little shopping around before you find what works best for you. I took an inventory regarding what I was looking for in a gym. I wanted a place that was conveniently located. There's nothing more discouraging than having to drive a long distance to work out; too many chances for mind changing. I wanted a place that had a decent selection of machines and free weights. I wanted a place that had a reasonably clean locker room in order to avoid diseases. By the way, watch out for ring worm; warm soapy water always works best. I wanted a place that played music that wouldn't give me heart burn and make me cry. I wanted a gym that had regular shaped members with decent dispositions. But most of all, I wanted a place where I felt welcomed. So I found a place that seemed to meet all of my requirements and signed up.

I signed up for three years because I discovered most gyms require this commitment. That's how they make their money; they make it on people who sign up, go for two weeks, but still have to pay because they signed. Hell, if all the people who purchased gym memberships went all of the time, there wouldn't be any room to move. Of course, you will be one of those that gyms don't make money on because you will go eternally. As far as being welcomed with open arms when you check in at a gym, forget about it. It is one of those facts of life: the people at the check-in desk aren't supposed to be friendly. I think they sign a contract to that effect. Just remember why you're there.

This new gym seemed to have it all, although it was a bit short on location. I had to drive a bit further than I would have liked. I started out at the first gym lifting a certain amount of weight, but after only six months I didn't increase it by much. (We'll get into all of that stuff about how much to lift, what machines to use and so on later.) At this new gym I increased the amount of weight I lifted, which meant that if I kept up with it I could expect to put on some positive muscle; and I did. I gained about five or six pounds during my time at this gym. It wasn't a bad experience at all. There was plenty of equipment to use; no waiting. There were even lots of cardio stuff like treadmills, stationary bikes and stairsteps. The music they piped over the loud speakers was tolerable. Lots of people who frequent gyms choose to provide their own sounds through the use of I-pads, iphones, blackberries, MP3's or whatever and portable CD players. I prefer not to bring my own music. I like to keep it simple; the less preparation and planning the better, I think. This gym even afforded the opportunity to meet some people and get acquainted. You get to recognize faces after a while if you have the opportunity to go at pretty much the same time every day; that's important if you can work it out. Depending on when you go dictates whether it is busy or not; not busy is the best because you have your choice of equipment.

Going to the gym at a given time every day can be crucial to your sticking with your routine. What I have discovered is the best time to go is usually mid-afternoon around 1 to 5 p.m. Anytime after that you catch the after work crowd. But even after work is okay because you get used to it; it becomes familiar; you learn what to workout on what day depending on how busy it is. And even if it is busy, the benefits you will derive are well worth it. This new gym was big enough so even when I did go at the popular time, I had plenty of options available to me.

As a college teacher I did have the option of using the facilities available at my school, which I did use on occasion. I would use them when I had to hang around for a faculty meeting; I used them when I was showing a colleague the ropes regarding workout form. But I didn't use them a lot primarily because the school's gym was usually full of students. Not that I don't like students; I sincerely do. I really don't believe one can be successful at teaching unless one truly likes students. I get along quite well with students and they find it comfortable to approach me regarding a class anytime they see me. I've even had students ask me a question when we were both standing at the urinal; each standing at our own by the way. And that's okay; I don't mind being there for them, but not when I am working out or taking a leak. I am there to get something accomplished and would rather not combine the two. Of course teaching at a school as big as the one I teach at I run into students and former students all of the time even the gym I currently go to. But even this new gym with all of its amenities only lasted about one year.

I think the main reason I stayed at this gym only a year was because of the location. It was a bit further than I wanted to go and was also in a location that made it difficult for me to exit when I left. Call me picky, but it occasionally detracted me from going and that's not good. A very important thing I did discover was that even though I stopped going to this gym they still expected me to pay up on my three year contract; be aware of that. Most gyms now do require that you commit to a minimum of three years whether you attend or not. Fortunately for me this gym went bankrupt not long after I changed gyms; I got lucky. No, I don't think it had anything to do with my decision to change gyms. I wish I had that impact.

The next gym I joined is the same one I continue to go to now. I've been a member now for almost 15 years. I did some research on the gyms available in my area. Any city of size today has more than a few gyms available for consideration; do your research. I found this gym one day when I left work from an entrance other that the one I usually took. It turned out to be less than five minutes from my work. This was great; I could be there within minutes of getting out of work.

This gym had all of the amenities of my previous gym including a convenient location. Another thing this gym seemed to have was a commitment to its members and a desire to continually improve. They seem to always be doing something to improve the conditions of the facility. They upgrade their equipment, keep the place quite clean, and play some fairly decent music over the speaker system. I found a home; it works for me. Now you have to find a home, a gym that works for you. Look around. Most gyms offer free introductory sessions and tours before you join. Get a free guest pass and try the facility out before you commit. They'll probably give you a sales pitch in the process; just consider that an opportunity to ask questions before you sign up. Remember, when you do sign up and make a commitment, go because it is your money, but more importantly, because it is your body. And don't tell yourself you will workout at home; you won't. For those of you who do believe you would work out at home, just remember and think about all of the distractions: the TV, phone, other people, and so on. Joining a gym gives that added incentive to go and work out.

Working out at home might seem like the best idea if you're busy like most of us are. I mean, look at all of the equipment you can purchase for home use. You can turn the TV on at any time of the day or night and catch an infomercial trying to sell you a piece of equipment they promise will change your life. Most of it isn't cheap. And it becomes even more expensive if you buy it and don't use it. How many of us right now have workout equipment gathering dust someplace in our houses? Quite a few I would suspect. I have about one hundred pounds of weight plates and various bars gathering dust in my spare room. I purchased the stuff with the best of intentions, but guess what, there are far more distractions in the home then in the gym. In the gym, we are there for one reason and one reason only: to workout. Occasionally, I must admit, I do use my home equipment if I have to skip the gym for personal or professional reasons. And I do use it, but my workout at home does not compare to what I do at the gym. I lift less weight and quit too early. A gym is where physical change takes place. Only you can choose to sculpt your body.

CHOOSING A GYM

1. Check the yellow pages or the internet
2. Visit the possibilities and take a tour
3. Compare member dues (the average gym charges between $30 and $65 a month; most also offer yearly memberships where the best buy can usually be had)
4. List your requirements: - clean shower/locker room
    - free towels
    - free weights
    - plenty of machines
    - cardio equipment
    - location
    - music/lighting/ventilation
5. Make a commitment

Remember that working out should first of all be fun. If you look at it that way you will succeed. One of my philosophies as a teacher is that education doesn't have to be a miserable experience. Somewhere, many of us were taught by someone to believe going to school should be equated with working: it is a big pain. Well, neither education nor working should be considered a painful experience. When we're taught to believe that, we enter with negative expectations. I believe everything we do in life, out of obligation or not, can be approached positively without hesitation or fear. Not only doesn't education have to be painful, it can be enjoyable and productive and a positive experience. It's just a matter of changing an erroneous attitude. Decide for yourself and make the best of anything and everything you do. Working out, exercising, is often regarded the same way. Some people have the preconceived notion that working out is a miserable, unsavory, painful way to spend 45 to 60 minutes a day. Well, they are wrong. It is not a miserable experience; in fact, the experience is very satisfying and fulfilling. But you won't know unless you try it for yourself .

CHAPTER 3

GETTING STARTED

Now that you've chosen a gym, there are a number of things you'll have to do before you start on your regular routine. I suppose if we were kids, all we would have to do is grab a pair of shorts, a tee shirt and be off for our work out. But we are middle aged men, not kids. So we have to use our intelligence and experience to get started in a positive way to ensure that once started we don't stop.

SEE YOUR DOCTOR

Seeing your doctor before you begin a work out routine is the necessary and practical thing to do. I know it sounds like something our mothers might tell us to do; that's because our mothers knew what was best for us. So you need to put the macho attitude aside and do what's best for you. Seeing your doctor is important especially if you're like a lot of men and just don't go to the doctor until you're bleeding, have a broken bone, hack up a lung, or are clutching your chest unable to breathe. It's the right thing to do. You need to have a complete checkup to ensure you get the most out of the gym experience. Don't take chances with your health; there is no percentage in it.

Your doctor can help you figure out what your capacity is; what you need to do to prepare for the gym. She can make suggestions as to how far you can push yourself and what sort of schedule you should follow the first month or so. So don't neglect your health. If you have made the decision to begin a work out routine, then make the decision to do it right: see your doctor first.

WARDROBE

One thing I always notice when I am at the gym is what people are wearing. I don't only check out only what the women are wearing, I check out what everyone is wearing. As far as wardrobe is concerned, my philosophy is to keep it simple; don't go overboard. Sure you can buy the spandex shorts, but I don't suggest it. Maybe you should wait until you've been going to the gym for a while before wearing tight, revealing shorts.

I feel some people put far too much time, effort and money into their gym wardrobe. The weights and machines are just as challenging whether you're wearing designer stuff or every day, good old reliable gray sweats.

CHOICES

Tank tops – various colors and styles (avoid tank tees - they make you look angry).

Tee shirts – without or without designs, messages (I prefer school tees: I have Harvard, Columbia, NYU, Monroe Community College - keeps people wondering). Or you could wear one saying, "I volleyball naked," so all of the women know you're obnoxious.

Shorts – one loose fitting, standard gym type shorts work best; sweats cut above the knee is also a possibility. Avoid spandex for the first year, or avoid shorts altogether if your legs are as white as mine and you don't want to scare people.

Pants – sweat or various kinds of workout pants made of nylon with zippers here and there.

Shoes – sneakers, preferably low top, any brand (I wear whatever I can buy cheaply: my kids call these bobo sneaks, but I don't care).

Hats – any type of standard baseball type cap will work, particularly if you're prone to sweating from your scalp like I am during humid weather. (Avoid sport team caps because other than yourself, who really cares who you're a fan of).

Sweat shirts – same advice as with tees. (People often wear these if they are either ashamed of the way they look, although they shouldn't be, or if they don't want to concentrate too much on progress during a workout. Masters of the Universe guys often wear sweat shirts for this reason – others aren't sure if they're really in shape or not).

Socks – white ones that don't fall down work best; they should be clean.

Underwear – who cares; no one will see anyway.

Weight Lifting Belt – I am in my late forties and have lower back trouble. (I don't take any chances when I am lifting weights). Can be purchased in most sporting goods stores.

Lifting gloves – used for achieving a better grip especially for those prone to sweaty palms.

Lifting straps – used for wrapping around various machines where pulling motion is the main intent; also used for those with grip problems like me. (I prefer these over gloves and they achieve about the same thing).

Lock – this is for the gym locker to store your stuff. Choices are either key lock or combination lock. (I prefer the key type lock because I don't want to memorize the combination. I have enough numbers in my head). I tie the key to the shoe lace of one of my sneaks.

CARING FOR YOUR GYM CLOTHES

You can carry your gym clothes back and forth in almost anything you want that you have around the house. For the first year or two I went to the gym, I carried my stuff in a regular plastic grocery bag. Hey, I didn't care what anyone thought, and it was easily replaceable. I go to the gym five to six times a week. I usually wash my stuff once a week unless it is in the summer and I am sweating more than usual and the clothes begin to get stiff half way through the week.

What I have in my gym bag on any given day includes gray sweat pants, two tank tops, one sleeveless tee, one hat, weight belt, sneakers and lifting straps. What top I wear often depends on what particular body part I am working and how I feel; do I want to see myself in the mirror today or not? It is just a matter of personal preference. The main thing to keep in mind is that you want to dress comfortably and practically. Always remember what you're going there to do.

Remember you're not at the gym to be seen or to socialize in the traditional sense. You are there to get in shape and to stay in shape. That doesn't mean you should avoid being social; actually the exact opposite should be the case; socialize all you want, but also keep your eye on your time. If you only have a certain amount of time set aside to work out every day, be aware of what you are doing with that time. So what you wear should suit your primary purpose.

Hopefully you've chosen a gym that suits you and what you are there to accomplish. What you'll discover is that there are quite a few people at your gym who are just like you; they are all at various stages of physical shape; there aren't a lot of people out there who wait until they get into shape before they will go to a gym. And those that do probably won't be going to your gym anyway.

WHO'S GOING TO YOUR GYM?

What type of people will be going to your gym depends a lot on what type of gym you choose to go to. Young people usually go to the type of gym that caters to their needs. Because most of them, because of age, aren't totally out of shape, one can surmise that getting into shape is not their first priority.

INTERNAL PREPARATION

So you have taken my best advice and decided to go to the gym right after work. What do you need to do before you go? Well, there's lots of stuff you can do before you jump into your car and head for the gym. You can pray; go to the bathroom; eat a Fig Newton, or five. The point here is, you will have to try a number of different things by way of preparing to go to the gym. I am mainly talking about what you put into your body at this point. Get a book on nutrition; speak with your doctor; strike up a conversation with someone at the gym who looks like he knows what he's doing. Visit a nutrition store like GNC. A word of warning here, although someone in the store might know what she's talking about, she's still there to sell you products; most sales folk don't have your best interests in mind. The key here is to find out for yourself. I won't leave you totally confused at this point; I will fill you in on what I do and did over the course of the past eight or nine years.

MY PREP

When I first began going to the gym with my son, believe it or not, I would stop home after work and drink a couple of beers. I certainly don't recommend that for beginners or advance gymers. I didn't know what the hell I was doing; I was only following the same routine I followed prior to my conversion. I quickly learned that drinking a beer before a workout was not a good idea. In fact, drinking anything carbonated is not a good idea either before you go or certainly while you are there. Carbonated beverages mimic food in the digestive system. Your digestive system works to digest that which isn't there; therefore you are expending energy you need for your workout. Not so with carbohydrate based foods. We all know that carbs give us energy; the energy we need for a good, productive workout. So, when I stopped preparing by drinking a beer and maybe eating a left over meatball, yeech, I tried lots of different things.

As we all know from all kinds of infomercials on TV, there are plenty of supplements available one can take in conjunction with a regular workout routine; but they are not cheap generally speaking. You can buy pre-workout energy drinks, post-workout recovery drinks. You can spend your money on energy supplements that promise to make you look ripped and manly. There are supplement bars available boasting up to 45g of carbohydrates. Some of these bars are made from chocolate, peanut butter, strawberry and so forth. The problem with these bars is eating one is like trying to chew off a piece of the sole of your shoe; you risk losing a tooth or two. But I have tried these bars and they do work; they do what they boast; you get increased energy that allows you to sustain your workout. But they aren't cheap; these bars can cost over two dollars each. And you have to take your time eating them, valuable time best saved for the gym. I still occasionally use them, but only when someone else buys them for me. Energy drinks are pretty good by way of prep.

Many of these supplements and energy producing concoctions do work; it's a big, money making industry. One energy source I do use on a semi-regular basis is Creatine as a pre-workout supplement. But even Creatine is not inexpensive. I don't suggest that as a beginner you use any supplements other than natural stuff found in food. Once you move from beginner towards advanced you can possibly consider a supplement. Just be sure before you buy something you educate yourself and read all of the literature you can find on a particular supplement, its effects and claims. Never put anything into your body unless you know everything you can discover about it.

CONSUME INTELLIGENTLY

What we consume before and after a workout comes from two different basic ideas of nutrition. I keep my diet fairly simple with my daily workout in mind. What is called grazing is a decent idea to employ during the day: eating a few little meals. What you should concentrate on here should be stuff that is mainly carbohydrate based. When I get up in the morning, for example, after I have a cup of coffee and let the stiffness work its way from my middle aged joints, and finish making those noises men make in the morning, I eat four or five Fig Newton's. Remember they're not cookies, they're Newton's. They taste pretty good and they give me energy I need to get my day going without feeling full and weighted down with a lot of crap in my stomach. I also keep some Fig Newton's at work. (No, I don't own any stock in the company). A bagel during the day is another good source of carbohydrates. Nutri-Grain bars are pretty good as well and have plenty of carbs and other good stuff to kick the energy up; and they come in a variety of flavors, too. Try to limit protein during the day because it will just decrease your energy. Like you know how you feel after a big holiday, or Sunday meal; you want to go to sleep. That's because you ate too much meat and fatty crap; so your body is telling you to relax and let it digest all of this heavy food. You should probably have your final mini-meal, snack, during the day about an hour before you go to the gym. Give your body a chance to convert the food to energy.

STAY AWAY FROM SUGAR--BAD, BAD STUFF

I used to be a refined sugar nut like lots of people. I was a slave to deserts; I craved ice cream and donuts. But I no longer eat refined sugar; and I no longer crave refined sugar products. I think a lot of it has to do with my regular work outs. My body has changed and sugar was a casualty. If you're not lucky enough to lose your taste for sugar, at least try to stay away from it before you go to the gym. Contrary to popular belief, sugar for most people is not an energy food; it is an energy zapper. There's a little test you can take to find out how sugar affects your energy level.

SUGAR TEST

- Get the old sugar bowl down from the shelf, and a clean tea spoon.
- Solicit someone's assistance.
- Put your arm straight out in front of you and lock it.
- Challenge your assistant to try to push your arm down as you resist.
- Hopefully you're up to the challenge and resist, or at least make it difficult.
- Now, put the spoon into the sugar bowl and retrieve a slightly rounded amount.
- Once again, place your arm stiffly in front of you.
- Place the spoon into your mouth.
- Again, challenge your assistant to push your arm down.
- If you are the type where sugar zaps your energy, pushing your arm down will be easier.
- If it is just as difficult as it was before the sugar, then sugar doesn't zap your energy.

You don't even need to swallow the sugar. We absorb refined sugar into our bodies right through our cheeks; that's part of why it tastes so good; everything happens the second we eat it. Either way, my best suggestion is to avoid sugar at least one hour before a work out. If you need a sugar boost, there are other, healthier ways to satisfy this hunger.

Now, I said I don't eat refined sugar, but that doesn't mean I don't use natural sugars like those found in fruits. One of the best, and healthiest fruits to eat during the day, and prior to a work out, is the good old fashioned banana. It has lots of good stuff such as potassium (guys, we need this) and vitamins D and C. I also eat apples, and pears, and peaches when I can get them before a work out. Even air popped popcorn is better for you before a work out than sugar. I also will drink a cup or two of coffee during the day; it's a stimulant and does help to keep the energy level up. But don't go overboard with the coffee; it's also a diuretic.

WATER

Yes, one of the best things to drink not only during the day, before going to the gym, and while you're at the gym, is water. Just regular old fashioned water: the kind you pay for or get from the drinking fountain. I wish I would have thought of putting water in a bottle and selling it for a buck or two; what a great idea. Anyway, your body needs water; we are mostly made up of water; and water replaces electrolytes we lose and need all day long. Always, always keep hydrated at the gym, whether you bring your own, or use their source, drink plenty of water. I never used to be a water drinker; I used to say water was only good for washing kids, cars and mixing with scotch, but I have since changed my mind. If you pay attention to what you put into your body during the day, and use your head in anticipation of your work out, you'll be successful and feel better for it.

AFTER THE GYM

No, this probably still isn't the best time to go home and have a couple of beers. Beer won't give your body what it needs following a good day at the gym. Although now is a good time to mention that the more muscle you have, the more calories you burn even when sedentary, and we all know beer has more than a few calories in each can. Protein is what you need following your work out.

There are plenty of after workout supplements you can buy to replace all of that stuff your body has expended during your workout. Protein drinks made from whey and other good things are really pretty good. Most come in powder form and can be mixed with juice, milk or water. I occasionally will purchase these drinks and use them; they work well and help to renew you after a good workout. I place a scoop or two in a glass and usually just mix it with water. But they are not inexpensive; most tend to run between 30 and 40 dollars for a gallon jug. Although when compared to how long they last, maybe the price isn't all that prohibitive. There are other, more natural ways you can replace nutrients and renew your energy.

One again, you need to drink plenty of water following your workout: need to replace those all important electrolytes. I didn't always know this. I rarely drank just plain water at all. I would get most of my fluids from coffee, the occasional soda, and occasional beer. One day at work I was explaining to a friend how I just felt like crap. You know, you get up tired, don't feel like doing anything and have little energy. She mentioned that she had a cousin who had been experiencing the same thing and her doctor told her she just needed to drink more water. The whole idea sounded rather simple to me; but I also thought it couldn't be that simple. Just for the hell of it I stopped at the drinking fountain on my way back to my office and had myself a drink. It was really weird; I immediately started to feel better. All it took was a little water; my electrolytes obviously needed replenishing. Try it. But there are also other things you need to do.

Don't worry about resting after a workout; your energy has been renewed. The last thing you need to do is sit down and take a good rest. Keep moving and doing whatever it is you need to do after. Take the kids for a bike ride; cut your grass (or mow your lawn if you're from the Midwest) build that bench, give your wife a tumble; give anybody's wife a tumble, just keep moving. Eat something after your workout, too. It should be something that is high in protein.

What I have found that seems to work best for me is eating whatever is left over from last night's dinner. Most people usually have some kind of protein portion to their evening meals. Open the frig when you get home and have a piece of that chicken; zap the cube steak in the microwave; hold a piece of halibut under your arm to warm it up. Eat something with substance after to renew what your body needs to recover. When you do resistance exercise, your muscles break down with the challenge and need protein to rebuild; that's how you get bigger muscles; you need to feed your muscles. If you don't eat anything that ever had a face because you're some kind of vegetarian fanatic, there are alternatives. I have a good friend who occasionally joins me at the gym who eats very little meat for health reasons more than anything else. (A secret: that's not a really bad idea, especially at our age. We eat way too much red meat, and it clogs shit up inside the body. That doesn't mean that you red meat lovers have to give it up; working out helps to compensate).

You can replace meat based protein with other things. Pick up some of that protein drink I mentioned earlier, it works. Beans, of all kinds, are also a good source of protein. I will occasionally buy a can of baked beans, open it and keep the beans in the frig. I will have a few ounces when I get home from the gym. For you sugar cravers, baked beans also help to satisfy that desire as well. Other choices include fruits, vegetables, cheese is a good one, and eggs. Egg whites are an especially good snack after a good workout. Of course, someone will have to eat the egg yolks because they are full of that cholesterol stuff that isn't really good for us in huge quantities. Hey, next time you have a big salad for dinner, toss the yolks in and spread 'em around. There are so many choices you can make; all you need to use is your imagination. The thing to do is to alternate what you use to renew. This includes even eating a Slim Jim once in a while after the gym. Think about it and keep it interesting in all ways, not just how you work out, but also what you do after.

WHAT TO DO

Okay there you are at the gym the first day. You pull into the parking lot and find a place to park right between the Mercedes and Nova. The sun is shining and right away you begin to experience the dreaded I-don't-want- to- go syndrome. It's too nice out; the birds are singing; my stomach hurts; I have to go to the bank; I forgot to clip my toe nails; I just can't miss today's episode of Oprah. Don't you do it; tell yourself, I got no place else to go. Walk into that gym with your head high and your skinny, drooping shoulders back. You'll be glad you did.

After you check in and make it to the locker room, pretend you know what you are doing; get changed into your gym clothes like you've been doing it all of your life. (Don't forget to rip the tags off your clothes if they're new). Don't worry, everyone is there for the same reason; they're not going to notice you as a novice. Just have a plan. Later in the book I'll offer a number of different routines you can begin with. Eventually, once you figure out what you're doing, you'll get creative to keep it fun.

Most gyms offer the services of a personal trainer to go around with you and show you what to do and help you develop a workable, hopefully productive routine. These people usually know what they're doing and can be quite useful, especially for the new guy. But they will charge you for the service; it rarely comes along with your membership. These one hour sessions usually run between 70 and 100 dollars depending on how upscale your gym is. It's not a bad investment; a way to get started. But you don't have to hire someone to show you how to do something you can figure out for yourself.

HOW I DID IT

When I started, I could little afford to hire someone; after all, I have three kids and bills and hobbies and habits. Besides, I am sure I would have totally embarrassed my son if I had someone going around with me showing me how to use all of the equipment and writing stuff down to record what I did. By the way, lots of people do that: they keep a running record of their workouts to keep track of progress and where they are in their schedules. It's not a bad idea at all; but once you really get into it, chances are you'll remember what's going on; if not, record it. What I did was just use logic. I was fortunate with my first gym experience in that I went to a place that was full of people who knew exactly what they were doing. I mean, you could tell they knew what they were doing. They were all puffed up with knowing what they were doing. What did I do? I watched them. I watched how they used the various machines. I watched how they used the free weights. I paid attention to their form. I paid attention to how much they lifted according to their size. I made mental notes on how much time they rested between sets and different exercises. As I watched others, I learned about symmetrical training. Symmetrical training is about working body parts that compliment each other. For example, when you do your back you are also working your biceps. So it makes sense to work your biceps on the days you're working your back muscles. I mimicked what the people who obviously knew what they were doing. Of course, I couldn't duplicate the weight they were lifting or setting on the machines; I had to compensate according to what I could handle. And it worked. If someone in your gym is in good shape, chances are he knows what they're doing and you can probably use him as a model. It's like having a personal trainer who doesn't know he's a personal trainer. Just avoid the people who don't look like they know what they're doing.

I don't suggest you be mean to them and soak their gym clothes in water and tie them in knots, and throw them out into the middle of the parking lot. Not at all; aren't we adults? What I do mean is to avoid emulating what they do in the gym. It's not too difficult to spot those who seem to be a bit short on effective technique. They are usually the ones you see at the gym on a regular basis who never seem to change physically; who seem to remain out of shape. They do seem to sweat a lot, generally from working too damn hard at doing everything they possibly can wrong. They do burn a few calories, but do little to build muscle. They practice poor form as well. Often they can be observed doing exercises on equipment in a scary way. You're not sure what particular muscle they are working. What they are doing is not necessarily working a muscle, but doing damage to their ligaments or joints. So, avoid duplicating their movements; you can certainly observe for amusement, just don't follow.

AFTER GLOW

It won't take long before you figure out what you're doing; have confidence and motivation. One day at a time is a good philosophy to follow. You need to pile days upon days and results will be there. Understand that your body is a complicated mechanism and requires well thought out attention. You can only really work certain parts at a time; proceed intelligently. More on routines later. Once a day has been successfully completed at the gym, you've done your 40 to 60 minutes; maybe a shower is in order.

Depending on your gym of choice, there are a number of possibilities here. A couple of years ago I went as a guest to a local upscale gym in my area that offered many extras my particular gym didn't. This is usually in direct relation to membership cost. This upscale gym charged twice what I paid for their monthly dues. The weights weren't any heavier; the machines weren't cushy; and the music wasn't any more inspiring; but you did get free towels in the locker room. Not only were free towels available (you couldn't take them home), but they also offered free shaving cream, cologne, various kinds of lotions, hair dryers, and a carpet on the locker room floor. Granted, these are really neat amenities, but are they worth the added cost? You decide; it all depends on what you require, and, of course, what you can afford.

If you're doing a lunch time workout, and are a sweater, a shower just might be in order. If this is the case, you'll have to provide your own towel if you choose a gym on the scale of mine. I generally don't take a shower following a workout for a couple of reasons. First of all, I don't want the other guys in the locker room to feel intimidated. I am just not comfortable showing off what I give myself and what is just there naturally, thank goodness. Hey, just kidding. I usually don't take a shower because I find it to be a big pain in the ass. I am fortunate in that I don't sweat, i.e. smell, a lot when I work out. I also don't want to have to worry about wet towels, did I pack a clean towel, and who the hell wants to be washing towels all of the time. I have a friend whose hobby is washing towels; so for him it's no problem; he has clean towels at his disposal all of the time. That isn't for me. I generally live alone and don't have a lot of desire to coordinate laundry more than once a week. But, hell that's me.

What I usually do after the gym is wash my hands with soap and warm water. You've been touching all kinds of things out there that a lot of other people have been touching and you don't know where their hands have been. Hell, sometimes I don't know where my hands have been. And we all know that one of the best ways to avoid germs is to wash our hands with warm, soapy water. I am not a germ freak, but better safe than sorry. I often see people in the gym who go a bit overboard with the germ thing. You'll recognize them; they're the ones who put various kinds of towels, paper and cloth, down on equipment where their heads and various body parts meet the surface. But there are also plenty of slobs who leave a piece of equipment or a bench with their sweat glistening in their wake. Some clean up after themselves; some don't. Most gyms, mine included, provide spray bottles and paper towels at various locations to employ for clean up.

Again, all I do is to wash my hands, get dressed, comb my hair, obsessively check my locker to ensure I didn't forget anything and skip out of the gym with freshness, and renewal. Give it a try. All you have to lose is some ugly fat and a habit for being inert. All you have to gain is your life back, and look good on top of that.

CHAPTER 4

MAKE IT FOREVER

CALL IT A HOBBY/PART TIME JOB

Once you do get started, it's important to stick to it and not let anything sway you from your course of physical renewal and maintenance. How far you go is certainly up to you; if you choose, you can put on a considerable amount of muscle weight if you are up to the challenge. I started working out at the gym weighing about 150 pounds; not bad for my height; but like I said before, I was not in really good shape. In fact, I can honestly say I am in the best shape of my life. Sure, the joints ain't what they used to be, but there are ways to compensate. I have, since beginning my exercise routine, put on about 15 pounds; that's 15 pounds of positive muscle weight. I know I could go further, but I choose not to. I have a decent, respectable physique. Once you get started, and know what you are doing, you just keep pyramiding up on the weight at intelligent intervals. Just don't get thwarted.

BODY TYPE

Everybody has a different body type; a different shape according to genetics. Generally we can't look to our parents to see what we would look like if we were in good shape because they often aren't in very good shape either. All you can do is the best you can. If you tend to be husky, chubby, fat like I was, then what you'll first notice as a result of your workout is a loss of fat, but not necessarily a loss of weight. Don't let this get you discouraged. If you're sticking to your routine on a regular basis, what you are probably doing is compensating the loss of bad fat with good muscle weight: muscle weighs more than fat. Pay attention to what you look like and how you feel, not what the scale tells you. In fact, I rarely ever weigh myself; if my pants fit and I feel good, then what's the point.

There is no set time frame that will tell you when you should start to see a difference in your physical appearance; it all depends on genetics and the extent of your routine. But I will say that you will begin to feel a difference within three weeks of beginning. Just don't get discouraged; that's why people quit; they get discouraged too damn quickly. Most of us are in such a hurry today to get things where we want them.

We're in a hurry to get into shape. We're in a hurry to make all the money we can to buy all the things we never really needed in the first place. Look at television today. If you have cable then you know what I am talking about. We have upwards of 200 channels to choose from. The internet and computer beckons us to waste time. How often have you sat in front of the box surfing for something to watch and not found anything? Why is that? I think we have too many choices. If we can't find anything, we slap a DVD into the old player because we don't want to wait to be entertained; we can't wait. We are a result oriented culture, but some things take time. Did you ever notice how all of the important things in our lives take time. Establishing a relationship takes time. Getting an education takes time. Raising a child takes lots of time. Building something well takes time; that's why building your body will take some time; give it a chance. Go ahead and hurry through making a meal and zap it in the microwave, rent a tape to watch, make that impulse purchase because you can't wait and need that stuff so bad, but take your time with your body. It will take care of you; it will be the only one you get. Treat it better than that car you're so crazy about; you can get another one of those. Did you also ever notice how when you buy something you thought you couldn't live without the thrill only lasts a little while? Well, being in shape can last forever.

Maybe your body type is the type with fast metabolism. Sure, you might not put on fat, but you also probably lack evident muscle structure. One of my friends who occasionally joins me at the gym is just this type. He eats whatever he wants but was perpetually thin. But he had absolutely no energy or strength. I recall when I was moving from one house to another he came to assist in the move. I had a set of 20 pound dumb bells on the floor of my bedroom. Out of the corner of my eye I noticed him bend down to pick them up to carry them out to the truck. He did pick them up for a moment, but couldn't quite straighten out. He quickly set them back on the floor and moved to a less challenging load to carry out to the truck. About five or six years ago he too started going to the gym on a regular basis.

This skinny, spaghetti armed guy had absolutely no idea what to do. For the next few months he followed me around the gym and basically duplicated my routine, but compensated for his initial lack of strength and lifted lighter weights. Within a few months, he was not only lifting those weights that gave him such a problem at my house, but he was using them for biceps curls. Now he is lifting weight that was once out of the question for him. He has renewed strength, more energy, and a new physique. Even fifty pound weights are no challenge for him on the dumb bell bench press. He does have a different body type than me, but he has developed the muscles his genetics allowed him to develop. His body structure is still on the lean side, but his muscle structure is quite apparent. Where once he was prone to keeping his arms covered when mowing the lawn, he now happily wears tank tops for the same chore.

The point is, no matter what type of body you have you can change it, but it takes time and effort. You didn't get out of shape over night; getting into shape will take time as well. Once you do begin to develop a new physique, you can feel comfortable knowing that muscles don't forget.

A few years ago, I found myself quite ill with a lung infection of some kind and found myself homebound for two weeks. Not only couldn't I go to the gym, I couldn't even go to the store to buy essentials. I had to rely on friends and family to do even my basic errands. I could barely move from the couch in my living room. I could barely eat anything to keep up my strength. It got so bad, when I called the doctor and he heard my voice he ordered me to the hospital at the risk of my very life. I went to the hospital and spent a week recovering and being treated for the infection. When I was finally discharged, the first thing I did was go to the gym. Big mistake. What I hadn't realized, was that not only did I lose 20 pounds, but I also lost the strength that went with it. I didn't have very much fat on my body to begin with, so the weight I lost was muscle weight. I smartened up and took it slow.

My physical recovery required the right nutrition and slow building up of my work out routine. What I mean when I say muscles don't forget is that if you lose time for important reasons, it won't take you as long as it initially did to reach your previous state. Your muscles remember where they were and are quite cooperative at rejuvenating to their former extent of development. After three weeks off, it only took me about five weeks to get back to where I was before I became ill. Where prior to that point, it had taken me a number of years to reach that level of muscle maturity.

Don't become discouraged if you need to take some time away from the gym for important reasons. Hey, most of us live busy lives with lots of important responsibilities that occasionally take precedent even over our needs. Just don't give up. I know from personal experience that when people miss a few days, or even weeks they might give up thinking What's the point. The point is you can always get back to where you were and surpass that level of development if you just don't give up. Even if you don't get encouragement from others, don't give up. By the time most of us have reached middle age we have even become invisible to certain people. Young attractive women kind of look right past us as though we didn't exist, maybe never did. But you can't become invisible to yourself. And even the young women might take a second look once in a while and give the old ego a big boost. You'll feel better about yourself and look better to others; just don't give up. Make your workout routine a part time job; think of it as an obligation that must be met. That's what I do. When I leave work and head to the gym I do it automatically like I was going to a part time job, or a kid's baseball game, or a dance recital. Most of us wouldn't think of missing something important to our families; so don't miss something that is important to you.

Make it a hobby. Everybody has something he does when he gets out of work to unwind and relax. Even if your hobby is watching the box, no one gets home from work and just waits for the next workday to begin. If you have a hobby, make this a second hobby. I know I always kind of envied guys who had hobbies, got enthusiastic about a passion. I would listen to guys talk about golf with such reverence and excitement and be a bit jealous. I even tried golf at one point in my life, but discovered I don't have the disposition to be good at it.

When I was in industry I tried a number of different things. For a period I was really into bicycling and all that went with it. I bought an expensive racing bike and subscribed to all of the important biking magazines. But my interest didn't last. Next I tried fishing. I would go to K-Mart and check out all of the neat equipment, fishing lures and poles and contemplate the strength of a line. But that also didn't last for me. For one thing, it generally required I get up too early and I don't operate well outdoors before the sun comes up. So, I allowed my subscriptions to fishing magazines to run out. Now I am really into photography and all that goes with it. I have even had some photographs published. It seems that I am sticking with this hobby, and I am also sticking to my workout routine. I also have a passion for reading and writing, but neither gets in the way of my working out. So whether you have a hobby, or a passion for an activity, working out can still fit into your life. And if you don't have a hobby, well great, this is one of the most enjoyable and beneficial hobbies you can have. Expand and renew yourself: be all that you can be and you don't even have to join the Army. Pick up some muscle magazines at the newsstand. There are all kinds available: from *Men's Health* to *Flex*; they cover all levels of interests and goals. They even offer lots of great tips and advice and suggestions for bettering and finding success in the experience of working out. Watch the progress of the people in the magazines and the regulars at your gym.

PEOPLE WATCHING

One of the things I like to do at the gym when I find my mind wondering, and one's mind shouldn't wonder when lifting heavy stuff, is watch other people. I rarely watch for technique tips now; I've been doing it long enough so I pretty much know what I am doing. But occasionally I pick up a new way of doing an exercise, or even a new exercise by paying attention to others. What I watch people for today is to classify, and try and read them without really knowing anything about them. Once you've been a gym member for a while, you begin to recognize the regulars who come at about the same time you do. Some you might even greet when you see them; some you will only remember based on something about their routines, dress or gym habits. Hey, what ever it takes to keep it interesting, and keep you motivated.

In the musclehead gym I used to go to I mainly classified the guys I figured I should stay away from; guys who might be prone to fall on me, or knock me down, or drop something on me. The gym I've been going to for about 20 years now has really become a great people watching gym for me. This kind of gym is the best kind. It's the best kind because all types of people attend; some come and go; and some come and come. Memberships, as far as I can tell, are split equally between men and women; that's a good thing. It's also quite diverse ethnically and culturally; that's a good thing. It's not uncommon to hear foreign languages spoken during a workout. My gym can boast members from all over the world; from such places as India and other Asian countries, Eastern Europe. There are Asians, East Europeans, African-Americans. I'm not talking about just a few people here; I'm talking about a largely mixed population. What does that tell me? Well, it tells me the world is a big, diverse place; it also tells me that working out, wanting to be in good, physical shape is something everyone wants.

I classify the people I watch into a number of categories: the beautiful people, the wanderers, the egos, the nuts, the serious, the confused, and everybody else. The beautiful people are those who are pleasant to look at and know it. They're not difficult to pick out of a crowd. They often wear gold in the gym. There is this one woman in particular who comes to mind and when you look at her you're not sure who to thank, the gym or God. She's attractive, tall, bosomy, terrific waist to hip ratio, and everything in the right place. She wears tight, spandex pants and some type of half bra top that accentuates her figure. She occasionally works out with a guy; I assume it's her boyfriend. He's a twerpy little person who doesn't deserve her. One day she was wearing quite a revealing get up and many of the male patrons were paying attention to her work out form. On the way out of the gym they were both noticing the attention she was getting and her boyfriend, who was walking behind her, reached around and covered up her breasts with his hands. They both had somewhat disgusted, arrogant looks on their faces as they walked away. My only thought was, what did they think would happen if she wore such a revealing outfit to work out at the gym? No one showed her any disrespect or even tried to have a conversation with her. Yes, she was beautiful; she dressed knowing how good she looked; and I assume she got the attention she wanted. Hell, nothing wrong with that.

The wanderers are a whole different group of people. They don't really do anything when they go to the gym; they just kind of wander. I think they might be there to meet people, but they just aren't sure how to do it. They come in with their gym clothes on and are usually carrying their gym bags right into the workout area. They usually stake out the same spot each and every time they show, drop their bags, stretch a bit, pick up the bag and wander to a new spot. I try to catch them using a machine, or lifting a weight, but it rarely happens. They wander, stop, stretch, and wander some more. Hell, some even bring their cell phones in with them and spend most of their time wandering and talking on the phone. Again, if that's their pleasure, nothing wrong with it.

The egos are the kind of people who are usually in really good shape and know it. Sometimes they're not in good shape, but have a terrific gym wardrobe. Either way, they are generally there to be seen, or get into the best shape they can. They rarely smile or say hello; that would indicate that you had reached their level, whatever that was. They pace quite a bit between exercises and sets, and make lots of noise. They grunt and groan and bang the weights around. They want to be noticed and try everything they can to ensure they're seen by everyone in the gym. They also spend a considerable amount of time in the locker room following their workouts. They do the kind of stuff I usually reserve for home. They shower, and shave, and powder, and spray, and blow dry. I even remember one guy standing in front of the two sinks totally naked clipping his toe nails into the sink. I suppose that's their gift to humanity. They're the noisy ones; the purposely visible ones.

The nuts are my favorite group to watch; there are all kinds of people who can fit into this category. I, of course, affectionately use the term nuts to describe these people. They don't seem to really have a plan at all; or they do - only they don't know it. This is the group that seems to be guided by rituals and habitual movements. They pace and touch and pace and touch. Often they can be seen working out on a machine, but they only work out on the one machine. They seem to be doing the same thing the whole time they are in the gym and everyday they come to the gym. You have to allow a muscle a minimum of twenty four hours rest before you work it again, but the nuts don't know that, or don't care. One guy has to go to the back of the gym every time he enters to touch the same place on the rear wall. He touches it, follows a pattern around the facility, and then goes back and touches it again. When he does a movement of sorts, he makes the neatest faces one could imagine. All of us make funny faces when we are challenged by the weight, but this guy makes the face no matter what he is doing; I bet he believes it's required in a gym no matter what you do. There are the other types as well, the ones who only work one or two body parts constantly. One guy who spends his entire workout time developing only his calves. Good calves are important, but along with everything else. This guy has great calves, remarkable calves, but that's all; the rest of him is pretty much unimpressive. (Maybe he wants to look like a professional bicycle racer).

At the risk of sounding judgmental, give me a break. All I'm talking about here are ways to keep your workout interesting, and even entertaining. You wouldn't be doing anything that everyone else in the gym wasn't doing. Hell,

I bet I fit into somebody's category. The rest of us, I like to think, will fall into the category you will of course fall into: the serious. We're in the gym to get into shape, feel good about who we are because, well, who else is gonna do it for us, and be in control. I believe it's important to take working out seriously, but also to make it fun and interesting so we keep going no matter what.

BODY PROTESTS

What if the spirit is willing, but for some reason the body doesn't want to cooperate on a given day or even a given week? Maybe our muscles are sore. Good. Your muscles will occasionally be sore if you're working out correctly. That's a good thing. Muscles get sore when they are challenged. The muscle tissue is breaking down from the strain and will rebuild when you rest that muscle. Deal with the soreness, get by it and keep it going. Deal with the soreness by giving that body part a rest for a day, or even better two. Try some over the counter pain relievers if you need to: Advil, Tylenol, good old aspirin, or whatever else works for you. If the muscle is still sore after a couple of days, then go easy the next time you work it...lighten up on the weights, use machines instead of free weights.

What if even the spirit is down in the dumps and the last thing you want to face is a challenging chest, leg or back workout? Then you just change your routine for that day. If you usually do the bench press with free weights, switch to machines for the day. Cut down on the challenge a bit just to ensure you get through your routine. Try a different exercise for that particular body part when the desire and motivation are limited. Give yourself the opportunity to try different things. This has the added benefit of keeping your muscles surprised. Alternating your routine is not only good for keeping up the motivation, it is also important to ensure you don't get to a plateau because your muscles are too familiar with your work out. Alternating and changing your routine is really positive for a number of reasons.

Don't allow injuries to get you discouraged either. We all experience various types of minor injuries no matter what we do. You can injure yourself just cutting the grass, or taking out the garbage, or yelling at your kids to take it out; that doesn't mean you won't do the grass or take out the garbage again. You just might do it a bit differently next time. Of course serious injury requires a doctor's attention. It all depends on what type of pain or injury you're experiencing.

Sharp pains, particularly those associated with the nerves or joints, do need attention. You know your body; read the signals it's sending you. I know as I close in on the big 50 my joints are not what they used to be; they occasionally give me trouble. My shoulder joints for example will no longer allow me to do what are called upright machine flies for my chest; my shoulders will no longer allow that movement without sending me a painful message. So I don't do that movement anymore. I compensate with a different movement that doesn't stress my shoulder joints.

It's important to convince yourself that just because you may be experiencing a bit of discomfort here and there that that doesn't mean you should give up on working out. I bet even Arnold has to compensate for his aging body. When something acts up, switch to machines, or free weights, try lighter weights, skip that particular muscle group altogether until the problem subsides; just don't give up. Chances are fairly certain that if you practice good form, and don't try and manipulate weight that is beyond your capacity, you won't experience an injury; just do it smart and listen to your body. And don't forget the good old fashioned over the counter pain reliever. Don't let your mind drift in the gym; you're just asking for trouble.

I don't remember how many times I had to assist someone and lift a barbell off of his chest because he had overestimated his ability. For many, the bench press seems to be the way they need to prove their masculinity. They'll walk into the gym for the first time, find an empty bench, and slab forty five pound plates on each end. They figure, if I can lift it to put it on the bar, I can press the two of them and the bar. They fail to take into account the fact that the bar itself weighs forty five pounds, and each plate weighs the same. The fail to realize they will be using their chest muscles almost exclusively with a bit of triceps thrown in. Unless these muscles are developed, they're in for a surprise. I remember this one thin man in particular pretty much emulating what I just described. I had never seen him in the gym before, but that didn't mean he didn't know what he was doing. He was rather thin; and I was curious enough to watch him try the movement. Never underestimate what people can do based on their physical appearance. Well, I could tell right away this guy had no idea what he was doing. He grabbed the bar with his hands too close together, lifted it off of the rack and held it there for a moment. As he lowered the bar to his chest, his arms were shaking a bit too much. When the bar reached his chest he couldn't push it back up. A movement like this is only effective if you can repeat the movement a minimum of 5 times. Well, the bar just rested on his chest; no matter how hard he struggled, he couldn't move it. I got up from what I was doing and went to his assistance. I enlisted someone's help and we each took a side of the bar and lifted it off of his chest and placed it back on the rack. I suggested to the young man that he might want to think about starting with lighter weights, or even a bench press machine until his strength was up to the challenge he just failed at. There are many ways to injure yourself in the gym, just don't let stupidity be one of them.

CHAPTER 5

OUR BODY'S JOURNEY

WHAT'S HAPPENING IN MIDDLE AGE

They say that before the age of forty a man can achieve an erection in under 10 seconds. I for one can attest to the validity of that statement. But I am not under forty anymore, and who ever said that was right; it takes me 11 seconds to achieve an erection. Don't I wish. It depends on a lot of factors for me. Am I alone? Am I with someone I find attractive? Am I with someone I know? Am I with someone I like? Am I in a crowd? Am I lost at sea without any water, or crackers? Whatever the scenario, it takes longer than 10 seconds; sometimes a lot longer. But the good news is, I always still get one, usually a pretty good one. Well, okay, not always. Most men experience some difficulty at one, or two, or more times in their lives. It's natural. Use it or lose it; that's true for many things in the middle years of our lives. Jack LaLanne, one of the founders of the modern era of exercise and leading a healthy lifestyle, was still active at 85 years old. Once he was asked if he used Viagra. "Are you kidding? I wake up every morning with an erection a cat can't scratch," was his response. And I for one am sure that, everything else aside, working out on a regular basis is to no small degree responsible for Jack's continued virility.

Hey, not that there's anything wrong with using Viagra if you need it, but why use it if there are other, more positive ways to get back to where you once were. Being out of shape, particularly in middle age, can have a rippling affect on our lives; it can affect many things negatively. Think about it; if you were or are losing your hair and devoting 45 minutes a day to some activity that would slow, even stop, the process of hair loss, wouldn't you do it? There's nothing wrong with wanting to increase your virility. It's just one of the many benefits of working out.

Remember the kind of erections you used to wake up with when you were 16? Hell, you could pound nails with it; it could open doors, close a drawer, make a sandwich. Well, working out may not get you back to that point, but it can help you increase your virility. There are all kinds of statistics available on men and virility and sexual dysfunction and their causes. Do the research, and one thing you will discover is that regular resistance training will reduce, if not eliminate the possibility of sexual problems now or in the future. It doesn't work for fetishes or fantasies, I will say. I still think about groups of naked woman with hairy underarms and attitude forcing me to perform show tunes. And that's one of my more normal fantasies.

There is change with time no matter what we do to try and stay ageless, but it can be limited if you do the right things. For example, through my forties I had absolutely no problem whatsoever having sex up to four times in an hour; I still fondly recall those experiences. Give me a minute; I'm day dreaming. Okay, I'm back. Now, in my late fifties I have been reduced to less success, but I'll take it. The way things are going now, I will be in my late 80's, early 90's before I am reduced to having sex according to the calendar rather than the clock. Of course, as we men know, this is all contingent on having someone around who is willing to have sex with you at all. We all know it, guys. Women have sex with whomever they want to; men have sex with whomever will let them. My philosophy is, hell I want to be ready all of the time just in case. Don't you?

GOT THE BLUES

By the time men hit middle age, even if their lives are relatively comfortable, they probably made enough shitty decisions, mistakes where they occasionally or more often feel depressed. Feeling down is inevitable and just another part of life. I've lost good jobs, screwed up a marriage, went bankrupt, have a daughter who had brain cancer, lost a mother, moved 8 times in 10 years and lots of other less stressful things to make me feel like not passing by open windows; but I persevered; I'm still here. I attribute a lot of my inner strength, my coping abilities, to, among other things, working out on a regular basis.

When my daughter was in the hospital fighting for her life I still went to the gym. I knew I had to be strong for her and my sons, but I still felt powerless. It really hit when she was rushed to the hospital almost a year after being diagnosed with a brain tumor. Her treatment was proceeding as expected, including having a feeding tube inserted to ensure she was receiving sufficient nutrition. Two months after that procedure, she was vomiting blood. There was a problem with the feeding tube. She had to be rushed into surgery to repair ulcers inside of her stomach. As all the medical people were hovering around her bedside quickly preparing her for emergency surgery, she motioned to me through the glass front of the room. She had the most terrified look on her twelve year old face. My heart broke. I ignored the rules and rushed to her side. No one really noticed me, they were too busy getting her ready. She reached her arms out to me between the hurried people. I clutched her tiny hands as I bent over her bed. With terror in her teary eyes she said to me, "What are we going to do now?" I was frightened, but wanted to appear strong for her. I said, "I don't know, honey." And what she said next changed my life; changed who I was. She said, "But you're supposed to know."

At that moment I realized how much our children depend on us, how much they need us. She wasn't reaching out to all of the doctors and nurses; she was reaching out to me for the answers, and I didn't have them. I felt powerless and without any control at all. She eventually came out of it, but it was a long haul; and continues to be a long haul, but she remains the hero, the light of my life.

Following that moment in the hospital, I wanted to destroy, blame, point fingers; I needed to cut the frustration out of me and feel real, normal again. So I went to the gym and lifted the frustration away; I sweated the pain into familiarity and hope for her, for me, for my sons. Not to make more out of it than it is, but lifting weights, pushing myself to my limits has saved my life more than once. Anyway, that's what I believe. Like I always say, It's better than pills (the side effects are positive) and cheaper than therapy.

There are plenty of medical studies that have concluded that vigorous exercise can have the same affect on how we feel as chemical substitutes. It can greatly reduce, or even eliminate depression. We're not only talking about the occasional bout with feeling blue; it also positively affects clinical depression. There are more than a few in the medical field who believe, that workouts may be just as effective as antidepressant medications in combating depression. I know it works for me and I'm not alone. As I've stated before, when feeling blue the last thing you might want to do is to go to the gym, but that is the time you should most go. You'll know you made the right decision not walking out of the gym; you'll know it while you're in the gym working out.

MIDDLE AGE GENETICS

It's usually in the middle years of our lives when whatever problems our parents might have experienced physically begin to manifest in us. We might not even notice the various changes taking place in our bodies, but the middle years are the best time we can begin to make a difference to combat what doesn't have to be inevitable. Men begin to lose muscle mass as early as the twenties; so by the time we've reached the middle years of our lives, we're mere shells of our former selves, but it doesn't have to be that way.

Not only can you stop the loss of muscle mass, you can reduce the natural loss of muscle that coincides with age. Most importantly, you can continue to build muscle for the rest of your life. Pay attention to your body to be sure that you're doing it correctly.

DURING AND AFTER A WORK OUT

Hunger Isn't An Issue -
If you begin to get hunger pangs before you're finished, your glucose levels are low, and you are about to use protein from your muscles for energy. In this case, you are shrinking your muscles. To avoid this, be sure to prepare prior to your work out by eating something with carbohydrates or natural sugar, the kind found in fruits.

Your Muscles Are Pumped -
A little while into your work out, the muscles you're working should feel pumped with blood: that's a real good thing. You can often actually see these results immediately during your work out. This blood pump releases lactic acid, and this is what results in muscle growth. Aren't you happy? This is a growth hormone that also zaps fat and pumps muscles.

You're Satisfied, Not Beat -
Your body will inform you that you've done just about all you can do for that day. Don't worry if you shake a bit when getting dressed in the locker room; that's

a sign that you have really worked your muscles in a positive way. The shaking will quickly pass; know that results are there.

You Feel Positive, High Almost -
Following a good workout you will feel good, probably the best you've felt all day. Your stress will seem less evident, or non-existent. What you've done is to release endorphins into your system, and it's endorphins that contribute greatly to feelings of well being.

Your Work Out is Smooth -
You have the same energy and overall strength throughout your entire work out. This means you have prepared adequately by eating and drinking the right stuff before you're rested; and there's been sufficient time between this workout and the last time you worked the same muscle group. If you're not feeling consistent, you probably didn't prepare, or warm your body up before you began, or you're not resting long enough between sets.

You're Encouraged -
If you did it right, you're looking forward to the next gym visit. It was all a positive experience and you feel the benefits. You go home and hug your family, make love to your wife twice and make lasagna for dinner. Note: if you are sick, don't go to the gym. You'll feel bad throughout the workout; will feel bad after, and probably won't look forward to going back. Don't sabotage your own progress and potential.

THANKS FOLKS

I lost my Mother when she was 74 years old. She wasn't even in the best of health when she passed away; hence that's probably why she died. Most people from our parents' generation didn't have the benefits that medical advances have afforded us baby boomers; and for many, it was partly due to lifestyle, that contributed to their deaths. But they also did have genetic considerations that we need to consider and pay attention to in order to ensure we live longer than they did. Research your parents genetic history regarding their health; heck, they are, or were, your parents, therefore you should probably know. My Mother had heart problems, as well as coronary artery disease; she didn't have the best diet throughout her life. My father lived to be 89. I think that was in part due to the fact that he was a nasty son of a bitch, but he also had good genetics.

I have had my cholesterol checked, as we all should in middle age, and it's great. My good cholesterol is around 69, and my bad cholesterol is 106. I attribute this, in part probably, to my father's genetics, but I also know for a fact that part of it is due to the fact that I work out. I know this because I have been told this by my doctor. Exercise and diet contribute greatly to lowering cholesterol levels. Working out on a regular basis also contributes to lowering blood pressure. Many people find themselves with increased blood pressure in middle age. Don't accept it just because it seems to be a fact of life; do something about it. You don't have to live with it; you can control your blood pressure through proper diet and exercise. Regular exercise has been proven to contribute considerably to the lowering of blood pressure. That way you can also avoid all of those blood pressure reducing side affects you can live without. It's up to you.

Not too long ago I had a touch of high blood pressure; nothing serious, just elevated. My doctor suggested that I incorporate more cardiovascular exercise into my workout routine. I had been doing a little, but obviously not enough. I increased the cardiovascular portion of my routine and lowered my blood pressure, and avoided having to take medication to control it. Exercising is good for you; it's good for the heart; it excellent for the quality of life, not only increasing the quantity.

REVERSE THE ABUSE

If you're anything like me, you've spent a fair portion of your life abusing your body. After all, didn't we always kind of feel we were immortal. But guess what, we're not. You can reverse the destructive process and live longer, happier and healthier. I spent far too much time eating lousy food, drinking and sitting on my ass, atrophying my body. It's never too late to become everything you were meant to be, everything you can be. But it's up to you to make the change. Project ten years into the future and ask yourself what do you think you wished you would have done ten years ago? Probably many things, but I bet working out will be on the list. Don't wait ten years to regret a decision you can make today. It's your body; it's your life.

CHAPTER 6

OUR MIND'S JOURNEY

Up to now I've been mainly discussing how to get our bodies into the shape they need to be so we can live happier, more fulfilling lives. It's true, when you're healthy, feel good, and look good life offers more opportunities for you to enjoy the moment and plan for the future. But, as I am sure we'll all agree, a healthy body is only part of a very complex equation. Many of us have not only ignored our bodies by the time we hit middle age, we have also allowed our minds to atrophy as well.

WHY?

Someplace, someone told us sometime that education, strengthening our intellects, was a tedious, painful process. And many of us bought into that idea. So we spent a good portion of our early lives hating school; trying to figure all kinds of ways to slide through and get it over with. We went because we had to, not because we wanted to. We hated our teachers, we hated studying, we hated homework, we hated tests, some of us even hated reading. Young boys were often made to feel inadequate intellectually, and we went along. It was regarded as unmanly if you were into school and studying. It was considered more important to be good at sports and win. So we played sports and won, and tried to act like we thought we were supposed to act: manly.

My father was gone by the time I was three years old; so I didn't have a male role model growing up. My Mother, trying to ensure I would grow up to be a man, signed me up for every sport going when I was young. She hunted down every intramural organized sport league in our neighborhood. I played basketball in the spring, baseball in the summer, and football in the fall. I even bowled on Saturday mornings. I was never very good at any of these sports, but I tried. I tried to preserver in spite of the humiliation, and the anxiety. I never even much cared if we won as long as I didn't make a total fool out of myself.

No one ever threw the ball to me in basketball; I played the line in football to keep me out of the way; I played rover in baseball. The position of rover has always fascinated me. It's a position that really has little use other than to keep the lousy players from screwing the game up too badly. I probably played baseball the longest. In the seven or eight years I played I improved very little until the final year. I never got to go to the playoffs, and ride the bus and stay in a hotel room and just have fun; I was never good enough. I was never good enough until the final year I played when I was about 12 years old. Prior to that I struck out almost every time I was up to bat; and I dropped the ball almost every time it was hit to me.

I think it was all of that practice at being bad that taught me how to really be good at the game. I never struck out my final year playing; I never dropped the ball. I was playing coveted positions in the infield, and batting cleanup for most of the season. I had the best batting average on the team, and I had never had a father as a coach in all of the years I played; I was always the kid without a father. And, of course, I never wanted my Mother coming to my games; that would have just compounded my humiliation. I was a player and I was finally getting slapped on the back. I was destined to be invited to go to the playoffs.

I can still remember the final game of the season; we won, of course. It was also the time they would announce those lucky players chosen for the playoff team. All of the teams from the league were gathered on one field for the reading of the sacred list. Cheers erupted when they began to announce the names; even though no one was really surprised at the selection. When my name was announced I did feel a surge of triumph; I had arrived; I was one of them. I still don't remember when I made the decision, or why. When everything had died down a bit, my coach came over, wrapped his arm around my shoulders for the first time and asked me if I was looking forward to the trip. I looked up at him as I was about to get on my bike to ride home and said, "No; I don't think I'm gonna go." And I rode home. When I told my Mother what had happened she thought I should go, but I also think she understood why I wasn't. My sister understood. She observed, was part of my growing up. She saw me struggle, and deal with disappointment. I think she saw my defiance as justified. She hugged me and I didn't try and wiggle away that one time.

Sports were just one part of what we were supposed to be as boys growing up in the fifties and sixties. Many of us didn't know what was expected of us in school; we knew we weren't supposed to like it, but I didn't know why. We knew we were supposed to behave and not cause any problems; I think we were just expected to be invisible and get through it. For me, maybe for many of us, school offered just as many if not more opportunities to feel as humiliated as in sports.

I went to parochial school up to the sixth grade; I remember that year the best. I think I remember that year so well because it was my last year there; I was asked, told actually, not to come back. It was also the only time I can recall a teacher in grammar school giving me personal attention. Sister didn't seem to notice, or acknowledge me, other than to point out my shortcomings. I was in the Brown Reading group; that was the group for the poor readers. It consisted of me and three other guys. During the in-class reading sessions, sister would usually spend most of her time with the Sky Blue Reading group, the girls, the good readers. I never understood: that if we were the poor readers and they were the good readers, shouldn't she have spent most of her time with us? I asked her that once and had to stay after school for having a smart mouth; a dozen times I stayed after school for having a smart mouth.

The one time I was afforded individual attention, I was staying after school for having a smart mouth. We were expected to keep busy and keep silent during these after school sessions. The other detainees usually consisted of the same guys from my reading group; we were used to it. I never did homework during these sessions; I spent most of the time making up stories, sometimes with drawings, sometimes without. Once, as sister was prowling the aisles of the classroom, she stopped at my desk and looked over my shoulder at what I was doing. "What's that you're writing, Mr. Brooks?" she asked, hands behind her back. I told her it was a story, and she asked if she could read it. She did; she read it all. She asked me questions about the story; she asked me questions about my writing; she asked me questions about me. I couldn't believe how good I felt. If she had only known.

High school wasn't much better. I was rejected by most girls until I met my future wife. My social life consisted of hanging out on the street corners with my friends doing nothing, but probably being a nuisance. I often think that had we had the benefit of malls to hang around, our social lives might have been better. But then we would have missed so much of what happens on city streets. We would have missed the afternoon drunks directing traffic, harassing the bookies coming around to pick up the numbers and the money. We would have missed the proprietor of the local candy store dumping water on his front step so we would have to move to another step until it dried. We would have missed the muscle cars cruising up and down the avenue. I just can't see a food court providing as much excitement as a street corner.

High school wasn't much of a challenge. I usually flunked every quarter; took the final and aced it and passed. I didn't even know I was in regents classes (often called honors in other areas) until graduation night when I was handed two diplomas. I often wondered why I was rarely in classes with my friends. Not many of my high school teachers stand out in a memorable way, except one. My shop teacher for 11th grade was Mr. P. He taught graphics, which I kind of liked. He spent a lot of time in the dark room smoking, but other than that, he pretty much left us alone to complete our projects. I remember him mostly because of his teaching style. When someone would ask him a question, he would look you right in the eye and answer, "You don't know do you?" And he would then walk away. I learned a lot from Mr. P.

I know I didn't read much in high school. I didn't do a lot to improve my mind at all. Sometimes I think high school is just a place to keep kids off the streets for a good part of the day during their formative years. We know where they all are and can go about our business without having to worry about dealing with teenagers. I did have hopes and dreams, but they kept changing; hey, go figure. It wasn't until my senior year when my counselor called me into his office for that obligatory what do you want to do with the rest of your life meeting.

When he asked me what I wanted to do now, I was lost for an answer. "How about college?" he asked.

"Okay," I answered.

"Where?" he asked as he thumbed through my file. "How about the community college?"

"Okay," I responded, thinking a number of my friends were going there.

"What would you like to major in; what do you want to BEEEEE?" About the only thing that my high school program would allow me to get admitted to was the accounting program. Why, I don't know, but he asked me if I would like to be an accountant? I remember thinking that I had an uncle who was an accountant and he seemed relatively happy, two cars, a house with a finished basement and all. So I agreed, having absolutely no idea what an accountant was or did. My math abilities were severely challenged, so I had no idea how I fit into an accounting program.

Needless to say, I didn't last, and ended up in the Army. I think that's one of the burdens men suffer from intellectually. We're always expected to know what we want to be, what we want to do; we always have to have some kind of plan. I mean how can anyone know truly what he wants to be, do for the rest of his life when he is 18 years old? It's ridiculous. So we end up going down the wrong paths and vegetate our lives away. But it doesn't have to be that way; it's never too late to change and become what you were meant to be even if that's just happy. But we have to do it as a complete package, the mind has to grow and become healthy right along with the body. It's never too late to stretch the intellect, and strengthen the mind, just like the body. But it has to be your choice; you have to put the effort into it; you have to find and hold onto the motivation to change and become all you can be. Actually when you think about it it's quite easy; you can do it right now. Are you ready? Okay, here it is: OPEN YOUR MIND. Now wasn't that easy. Well, maybe not as easy as we wish, but not as difficult as we may have thought either.

READ AND GROW

Remember those things you probably never picked up in school if you were anything like me...books. That's always a good place to begin: read a book or a thousand. You have heard it before I am sure...a book can change your life... but it's true. It's all about exercising the brain. Sure, you're probably saying, of course a college professor would be encouraging reading. Mark Twain said, "The person who chooses not to read has nothing over the person who can't read." No, it's more like a middle aged baby boomer who's encouraging reading and exploring. Do you want to expand your muscles...good, now get ready to expand your mind, too. Make it a complete package. When you think about it, everything we acquire in life can be taken away from us: we could lose our jobs, our home; our wife could run away with a bartender; your golf clubs could be stolen on the day the IRS is auditing your tax returns for the last 11 years, but you can never lose, no one can ever take away from you, what you have given yourself intellectually. That's yours forever.

When I was in the Army I had to go on twenty four hour guard duty and I was looking for something to bring with me to read. A friend had a book sitting on top of his foot locker and I asked if I could borrow it. I didn't even know what it was when he handed it to me. I liked the cover, two fingers extended in the peace sign. I read the book twice during that twenty four hours on guard duty. I couldn't put it down; it totally changed my life. The book was *Johnny Got His Gun* by Dalton Trumbo. That book opened my eyes to many things I thought I knew, many things I was confused about, many things I never thought about. Reading that book was a revelation for me; a life changing experience. I began to look at myself differently; I began to look at and consider others differently; I looked at life differently. This book, along with a suggested reading list can be found in the index.

Johnny Got His Gun made me think; and anything that truly has value to our lives makes us think. We are confronted with so much external crap today, crap that doesn't require us to think, that we sometimes have forgotten how. I'm talking about real thought here; not just recalling, repeating, or duplicating but real thought. The questioning kind of thought that leads to revelation and exploration and dreaming. Most of what we are exposed to in the media requires very little participation on our parts. We are only required to sit back and be present. The movies we go to, the television we watch, the computers, cell phones we stare at for hours, the books we read are all basically familiar; there is little if anything that is unpredictable about what we choose to entertain us.

Real thought comes from exposing ourselves to things that don't provide all of the answers, offers us questions to ponder. This is how we expand our intellects and grow as human beings. Most of the movies we pay to see, or rent, provide one thing and one thing only: time consuming entertainment. Don't get me wrong, there is nothing wrong with being entertained; but we also need some good stuff in our diets as well. Did you ever eat fast food late at night and wake up the next morning feeling as though you had a hangover? I have; and there's a reason for that. If all you ate was fast food you'd feel pretty shitty most of the time. The first part of this book dealt with taking care of your body, being reasonable and responsible with your health. We should also have the same plan, attitude about our minds. Most popular movies don't require thought at all; they are familiar and predictable.

When you go to see a James Bond movie you know exactly what will be in it; it will have fast cars, beautiful women, neat gadgets and a nasty villain. You will also know even before it starts how it will end: Bond triumphs over evil and scores with the girl. But many people go anyway; we go to be entertained to the conclusion. If half way through the film Bond confessed to being gay we'd be shocked. We'd turn to the person next to us and ask if we heard right. We wouldn't expect that; that would be too unpredictable. Not that there is anything wrong with James Bond movies, but you wouldn't go to a coffee house after to discuss the sociological ramifications of the plot line, or characters' motivation. You wouldn't because all of those answers were provided in the film; you're left with nothing to ponder other than the cost of the ticket.

There are certain popular actors who keep making the same movie over and over again; and we keep paying to see it. Take the popular five-part or more boxing series that began in the late 70's. All five movies are pretty much the same. The main character is faced with a formidable challenge that he is not quite certain he is up to. He needs inspiration to see him through, to guide him to triumph; and he gets it. Did you ever notice in the first film how this character was a bit stupid, with a limited vocabulary, and how with each subsequent film and the earning of more and more money he gets smarter. Well, by the fifth installment he has lost all of his money and he is stupid again. Some positive message there, right. And we always know he will win in the end: that's entertainment.

But movies are certainly not hopeless; there are many fine movies being produced that do require intellectual response. Unfortunately, they are not always as popular as the big blockbusters. There is generally a reason why a film wins an academy award, generally; it's because it's a good film. These are the type of films that do require thought. Most films only require an emotional response from the viewer; we respond by laughing, crying, being afraid, being stimulated or whatever; we don't respond intellectually. The films that require an intellectual response on top of the emotional response are generally the best films; they have artistic integrity. The 2000 winner of the academy award, "American Beauty," is a good example. The movie "The Road" based on the Pulitzer winning novel grabs me by the heart it is so powerful. The movie left the viewer questioning many things, including society, values, and loyalty. Watch a good film. Explore the unpredictable; exercise your mind. Our minds require a balanced diet just like our bodies.

Television is yet another source of entertainment for all of us, myself included. Everybody watches TV; it is part of American culture. I grew up watching TV. I can still remember my favorite shows as a child: "Kukla, Fran &

Ollie," " The Howdy Doody Show," " Leave It To Beaver," and the" Mickey Mouse Club." Some might debate the point, but these shows were offered purely as entertainment; they had no intellectual value, but that's okay. Kids need to be entertained; hell, adults need to be entertained. I think we just spend far too much time in front of the TV today, and in front of the computer, and we can never get that time back.

Just like most of the movies we watch, most of what we see on TV is predictable and familiar; you know what's going to happen before it happens. Life isn't like that; TV ain't real. Life is not predictable. Like the philosopher said, "we make plans, and God laughs." True art mirrors, emulates life. We learn from the questions we ponder; we strive to discover answers, we learn. Most situation comedies on TV today are just another form of entertainment; they have absolutely no intrinsic value. They are usually 23 minutes of entertainment that does one thing and one thing only, take up time. Hey, back to this time thing. Why are we, again, in such a hurry? We want to be done with school, get out of work, retire. Why? So we can spend more time watching TV or surfing the net? Let's hope not.

Watch TV if you have to, but balance your viewing diet; expand you intellect every chance you get. Turn to the Discovery channel, the History channel, your local PBS channel; expose your kids to the choices they have, the possibilities life offers. Give yourself and your family the gift of thought. There are even some popular dramas on TV that have some value. One of my favorite old shows over the years was a hospital drama called, "St. Elsewhere." You might or might not recall it. It was where a number of popular actors today got their start, including Denzel Washington. The show was loaded with metaphor; it truly required intellectual participation. What TV shows do you hear people discussing at work the next day? They are usually the ones that require a little effort, some brain exercising; give them a try. There is some good, valuable TV out there; you just have to find it. Influence your kids; turn it off or turn it to something worthwhile.

Most of the really bad, and I mean bad TV, out there today revolves around the premise they we are, in part, a society of voyeurs. Reality TV has really gotten out of control, although I do think Snooky is amusing. We love to watch other people discuss their problems, see them in conflict. Think about the popularity of all of the news shows, talk shows, real world kind of stuff. We want to always feel better about ourselves, so we watch people who are worse off than we are; we like to think they are anyway. One of my worst nightmares is waking up at two in the morning, looking out the window and seeing "The Cops" show setting up lights and cameras in front of my house. But I still watch it once in a while, as I am sure many people do; that's why it's still on. And why are most of the people they arrest toothless, drunk and in their underwear? There's some food for thought. I'll leave it to you to ponder. And why do people go on those talk shows to expose their lives?

They go on those shows because that's the only way they can see in their miserable lives of being treated as though they are important. All they have to talk about is how they fell in love with their sisters, cheated on their spouses, or hate certain people. I say give them a pill, not a limo ride to the studio. We all know the world can be a very cruel and sick place. But do we have to be constantly reminded of that fact? No. All of the news shows, talk shows, expose shows, real life shows are only distractions for our lives. They don't even really have any entertainment value. They might make us feel better about who we are, but they do that for all of the wrong reasons. We should feel important because we love and take care of our families, are good to people, not because there are others out there who are worse off than we are. Turn the box off and pick up a book. Exercise your mind and pump up your intellect. And who really needs to keep up with the Kardashians?

READING IS FUNDAMENTAL

Just like maintaining a healthy body is fundamental to a complete life, so is reading, exercising the mind. As I have said before, I didn't grow up as a reader; but fortunately for me I discovered the value of the written word. It's not that I didn't have positive influences in my early years; I just never noticed. My Mother would get up an hour early every morning before she had to go to work, and sit at the kitchen table reading. I guess I just never paid attention; but in retrospect I suppose it was kind of a silent influence that just took a while to hit me. Again, it's never too late; whether you start reading at 18 or 58; pick up a book, a good book. Like Mark Twain said, "The man who chooses not to read has nothing over the man who can't read." Or something like that.

Just like I was saying earlier about some movies having intellectual value but most don't, the same is true when trying to decide what to read. There is plenty of reading material available that does a variety of things for us. You can read the newspaper for news; magazines give the reader usually a more in depth look at the news of the day. What comes from reading the news? Well, other than consternation, you get the news and that's all. You know what the newspapers think is important for you to know; it's their choice, not yours. It's the same with magazines that have mainly an entertainment focus. You read, and learn about what the editors think you should read about and know. You get the latest gossip on celebrities (who gives a shit), politicians, and popular issues of the day. Any intellectual value in this stuff? Not much. It's just like watching a movie that merely entertains; you've spent some time being other directed. Maybe that's some of the time you've been saving up to do something important. Again, it's all a matter of having a balanced diet; in this case, intellectually.

Reading something of value does take some commitment; it's not as easy as reading the daily newspaper; it requires that you pay attention and think. That's where the growth comes from. Who's to say what's good, what has value. Well, I suppose when it comes right down to it, you are. But there are ways to tell if something you're reading has intellectual value for you. Does it require that you pay attention? Do you find yourself thinking, contemplating the issues the book addresses? Are you more often than not left with more questions than answers? If one or all of these points are in place, than you have grown intellectually; your mental muscles are getting bigger.

FICTION/NON-FICTION

Neither fiction nor non-fiction have value over the other necessarily. Generally works of non-fiction provide information, whether it be biographical, historical, self help, informational, how to, or whatever. A well written, challenging non-fiction work can certainly have intellectual value for the reader. But non-fiction is not in the truest sense art. And it is the art of fiction that provides the best, most rewarding opportunities for intellectual stimulation and growth. The contemplation of art is the free weight routine of the mind. Kind of a dumb analogy, I know, but what the hell. But is art in the eye of the beholder?

Well, many of my students think it is, think that art is totally subjective. And in a way, they are not totally wrong, just a bit incorrect. True art has an intent; the artist intended to achieve something; to make a statement that could be discovered. But it isn't always easy. This is where we can also discern what is good, from what is not good; in that, it lacks artistic and intellectual value. For example, is what Stephen King writes art? Well at the risk of offending some, no, it isn't. That's not to say that King isn't a fine writer; he is. Not that he needs me to praise him and tell him to keep up the good work. He does just fine on his own. What King writes is entertaining, emotionally attractive for the reader. When you read something by King, you respond emotionally, but not intellectually. He scares us; frightens us often out of our wits, and that's fun; that's extremely entertaining. It is not difficult to discern what King is trying to accomplish; it is all kind of familiar and predictable. I can honestly say King has written some stuff that I believe has intellectual, artistic value. Novellas like "The Body" and "Rita Hayworth and Shawshank Redemption" and the nove *The Green Mile*, a good try at a Messianic parable, and others are very well done. But that's not what he usually chooses to write. He is best at entertaining; not that there's anything wrong with that. You read King's stuff and you get it; it's pretty much all there.

But that doesn't mean that you always have to get, to understand everything you read totally. It's in the challenge, the effort where growth takes place. We don't have to understand everything in life; not everything has to be totally clear for us. There might be a reason for everything, it's just that sometimes we don't know what the reason is. It's like trying to understand a person. People are always a good analogy to use when discussing, and trying to understand art. You see a person you think is attractive, and you would like to get to know her better even if only in a platonic kind of way. So you spend some time with her and discover that she is confusing; you just don't understand her, her motivations, beliefs, anything about who she is. That doesn't mean you reject that person; the person's value may be in the challenge of getting to know him or her, and what that person is all about. It is worth the effort. It's the same with art, a good book is worth the challenge of trying to get to know it, and understand what it's all about. Don't give up because it makes you think; accept the chance to grow. Don't tell yourself you don't have time to read something good; you've been saving up time all of your life, and now that we are middle aged it's about time we used that bank of minutes and hours to accomplish something really positive. Don't know what to read? Check the appendix for a suggested reading list.

CHAPTER 7

BACK TO THE BASICS

IMAGINATION

Remember when you were a kid and you could spend hours alone without anything electronic to occupy your time? All I needed when I was nine years old on a Saturday afternoon was a spoon from the kitchen drawer and I was set. I could dig to China, build roads, make a city come alive, and extend myself beyond my tiny little world. I could use my imagination to be anything I wanted to be, and go anyplace I wanted to go without worrying about super saver prices, or air miles. I fought and helped win World War II in the Pacific and in Europe. I was instrumental in the westward expansion; I served in Washington's Army; I fought to free the slaves in the Civil War, and when the day was done, I slept the sleep of a child, and dreamt of tomorrow. What happened?

Now that we're middle aged, we don't go out into the back yard with a spoon anymore; we don't run around the neighborhood playing Army (we'd probably get shot today), and we no longer know what it's like to sleep the sleep of a child. For many of us, our imaginations have atrophied. We escape by going to the movies, by watching television, surfing the internet and by regretting the dreams we had for tomorrow. We have lost the ability to escape into our own thoughts and find inspiration in our imaginations. But just as we can rebuild our bodies and our intellects, we have the power within to rebuild our imaginations; to realize the power that's always been there. Like the Great Wizard of Oz knew, we have always had the power to go home; we just never knew it; or was that Glenda the Good Witch? If you remember, then you're on your way.

What happened to our imaginations? I suspect we baby boomers were encouraged to act grown up before we were ready. Day dreaming, thinking on our own, imagining that which never was, all that stuff was not practical for the real world; or so we were told. Our lives can be filled with good and bad memories; we store them away; all we are is memory; that is who we are. Many of those memories, for me anyway, are of childhood, and times my ideas and thoughts were oh so new, and all mine. Now we think what we are presented to think by others, whether they be in the media, or those we are responsible to. Recently a student said to me, he didn't have to remember anything because he had access to the internet on his phone. That's just all kinds of too bad. But not necessarily a totally bad thing, but that's not all there is; thinking is also fundamental. Dust off the imagination, and act like a kid once again; at least once in awhile.

Remember when you were a kid and could talk yourself into being scared just because you heard a noise outside late at night. You'd be in bed in the dark and would hear a scratching sound coming from outside of your window. The more you heard it, the more afraid you would get. And before you knew it, you had the covers pulled up over your head and you were sure there was some kind of monster about to enter your room. It was usually just a branch scratching up against the house, or maybe a real monster. The point is, it was your imagination that encouraged you to react. Remember when puberty hit, and I mean hit hard? Well, tell me another time the imagination proved more valuable, especially considering the fact we couldn't get a girl to come near us for love or money at that age. Hell, all we had was our imaginations and the Sunday paper underwear ads. Try to remember some of your fantasies from then; weren't they the best? Each and every one of us has had something terrible happen in our lives; hell, you get to be our age you can't avoid it. All we would have to do to be sad is to call up that memory and live with it for a moment or two. Again, that's the power of the imagination. What did you enjoy doing as a kid; make a list. Do it again, but be careful who might be watching.

I remember how on warm summer nights I would go outside and lay down on the grass and look up at the sky and just imagine what was out there. As adults we watch "Star Wars," or something like that, and allow someone else to tell us what they think is out there. Imagine yourself; you can entertain yourself much better than anyone else. Well, I still do that and don't care what anyone thinks; it can be quite relaxing, better than a beer or glass of wine. Go outside with your kids or grandkids and play a game with them like you used to do; get down on the grass to their level and smile and laugh. We've all been acting like adults long enough; it's time to act like a kid again and drop the barriers we've constructed over the years. We don't see ourselves as other do anyway.

ART IS EVERYWHERE

"Truth is beauty, beauty truth. That is all ye know on earth, all ye need to know." Keats, "Ode to a Grecian Urn." Art, the beauty life has to offer is right in front of us for the taking; for the contemplating. Expanding the intellect, becoming who we can become can happen each and every day of our lives if we just open up to the wonder and beauty the world has to offer. One of my favorite things to do on a Saturday afternoon is to visit an art gallery. I love to just stand in front of great works of art and just think; I think about the artist's motivations, the intensity of the subjects and, most importantly, how the work makes me feel and what it makes me think about. Hemingway use to go to art museums and just stand in front of paintings for hours on end. He would take in every subtle brush stroke, every hint of light and learn. He used this method to describe scenes in his novels and short stories. In case you forget, he did win the Nobel Prize for literature.

How often can you go to the same art gallery? You can go as often as you can. Never mind that many of the works you see are the same ones you saw on your last visit; you're not that person anymore. Every time you experience something, you are a different person, capable of a different, experienced interpretation. How many times can you watch your favorite movies? I know that some of the movies I really enjoy I could watch over and over again; that's probably why we buy the DVD's. We can watch them again and again because we are different each time we watch. Bring someone with you to the art gallery; that will make it a brand new experience. Share the beauty you discover around you. And don't worry if you look at a painting, or read a book and just don't get it, can't quite figure it out; it's the experience that counts, the intellectual participation.

One of my favorite artists is Vincent Van Gogh. I love what he was all about; I love the beauty he created; I love the imagination his work was born from; I love the challenge of trying to see into his soul. Van Gogh lived poor and he died poor, but that didn't keep him from his work. He had to paint; creativity is a necessity in all of us. Don't believe me? Think about all of the effort you put into that deck you built in the back yard, the chair you repaired, the garden that smiles at you, the meal you cooked. I love to live with Van Gogh's "Starry Night" and try and imagine what he was thinking. Was his genius twisted or just beyond my grasp. I love to watch the beautiful colors, and shades of light he used in "Irises" and contemplate the brightness of his genius. I love Gauguin and the simplicity and power, at the same time, he created with many of his paintings done in the South Pacific. I appreciate the intellectual challenge; the invitation art extends to me each time I have the courage to take a chance and go beyond the familiar. I may sometimes walk away confused; but I also walk away alive. Art is all around us; beauty and the imagination are all around us; we just need to open our eyes and see what's there. Read McCarthy's, *The Road* and see if you look at a tree or flower in the same way as before.

It's so easy to become complacent with life and just go through our daily routines. It seems we're always hurrying to get from point A to point B just to feel some sense of accomplishment. What we often end up doing, especially by middle age, is ignoring all of those things around us that once held wonder and challenge for us. I marvel at people who walk around with those day date books, ipads and phones keeping track of every minute of their days, where they have to be, when they have to be there. For a number of years, I would buy one of those day date minders and vow to keep track of what I had to do. I would usually be fairly diligent through the first month or two of the year, then I would slide and stop jotting stupid little reminders down; so I stopped. I figure if it's important enough, I'll remember what I have to do; if I don't, well, then, that's the name of that tune. Life should be full of surprises. It's like, if you know everything that is going to happen each day, what's the point of getting up in the morning. It's like watching a TV rerun you didn't like in the first place.

READ A POEM
When I was a kid, I would get up at 6 A.M. every Saturday morning to watch three hours of the "Three Stooges;" one of my favorite shows at the time. I suppose, it was a favorite of most guys when they were young. I would lie on the floor without moving, except to go to the bathroom, until every episode was over. During the commercials I would divert my attention but stay ready for the next Curly, Moe, and Larry

episode. One morning I noticed a book propping up one end of our couch. During a particularly long break, I grabbed the book and yanked it out; the couch teetered. It was a paper back collection of American Poetry.

I thumbed through the book while the commercial played and even paused to read parts of some of the poems. I put the book back following the commercial, but often took it out after I discovered it. I would occasionally find myself exploring the collection even before I turned on the TV. That was when I discovered Frost and Whitman and many others. We only had three channels; so the chance I was really missing something was pretty remote. Except on Saturday mornings, of course. I couldn't miss the Stooges, "Sky King," "My Friend Flicka," "Bugs Bunny" (from whom I learned sarcasm), and all of the rest of my favorite shows. But when I did read it, I actually found myself enjoying it. I discovered Frost and Whitman, and the Expatriate Poets from Hemingway and Fitzgerald's Paris, like Ezra Pound, and William Carlos Williams. I didn't know that at the time of course, but I read them just the same. When my friends would come to call I would quickly put the book under the couch; couldn't let them know I was reading poetry. It wasn't a manly thing. That was then; this is now. Poetry can be like a beautiful painting, but without colors. Poets paint wonderful pictures with words, something I have always been fascinated by, although I spent many years denying and disregarding that because I was too damn busy saving up time and working to buy crap.

Poetry is an art form that is too often ignored in this country; maybe that's because good poetry requires thought. Most of us middle age baby boomers don't find poetry familiar and comfortable; it's too unpredictable for us. But it doesn't have to be. I now teach a contemporary poetry class; it's not even like working, sharing the beauty of language with students. Many times students will come up to me toward the end of a semester and express gratitude regarding, for many, their introduction to poetry. They often will express,

"I didn't know what I was missing." And many of them are students who never really paid attention to a poem even when they were supposed to in high school. Give yourself the gift of poetry. Three former Presidents I really admire are the only ones who had poets recite at their inaugurations: Kennedy had Frost, Carter Had Dickey, and Clinton had Angelou. These are three terrific poets to begin with.

Poets can help us to discover meaning in our lives; look at things from a different point of view. Poetry can absorb, inspire and encourage understanding. Even if you read a poem and don't get it, that's okay. Remember, the value is more often than not in the experience of exploration, not in always reaching the goal. There are numerous anthologies of poetry available in most any book store. Anthologies are usually collections of a variety of poets and their work. A collection is generally a bunch of poems from a single poet. Explore and discover what poets reach you, make you think, and shine a little beauty into your life. But try and read good poetry. Again, if you don't get it, don't worry; it's like the song you've been hearing for years not knowing what it was about, but just enjoyed the sound of it. Enjoy the sounds of poetry.

I guess the definition of good poetry is probably poetry that challenges, opens your eyes, paints a picture with language you've never seen before, or felt it just the same way. There's a lot of bad poetry out there and we read it regularly. When you go into the drugstore to buy a card for your wife at the last minute, you're usually reading bad poetry. It only deals with emotion, nothing concrete; it fails to challenge the intellect. I know how it works; I do it all of the time. I pick up card after card for a loved one's birthday, Christmas, Valentine's Day, and finally find the right one. Sometimes I even get a little misty reading the poem and thinking about the person I want to give it to. I'm only responding that way because I know the person and how the words in the card fit how I feel about that person. A good poem has to exist beyond the poet, and beyond only an emotional response. A good poem has to be about something; a poem about love is only about an emotion; it has little concrete value. Poetry has to have images that flood the mind with wonder and question and beauty.

WRITE A POEM

We are all poets. We see poetry in the eyes of our children, we feel poetry in the touch of our wives, girlfriends. We live poetry when we contemplate pain in the world and wonder why. Write a poem about something. If you feel love in your life, write a poem that even a stranger would be able to experience. I write poetry; have even had some published. Not too long ago I was inspired to write a poem about love, but not just the feeling. So I wrote a poem about how my daughter used to help my Mother up the stairs because her arthritis was so bad. That's love. Someone who doesn't know me can see and experience that sense of love without ambiguous emotion getting in the way of the reality of love. Something happening is more real than just what happens. What happened when my daughter helped my Mother up the stairs was an expression of love, but the happening of her helping is the truth of that love, the manifestation of it.

You want to write a poem; write a word on a piece of paper; write the word 'Perhaps'...and take it from there. Poets think in lines; where you break the line can be very important. Each line can be like an image, a photo if you will. And the poem itself can be a series of images that paint a story, reveal a panorama. Poetry, as well as stories in general deal with truth. And it is only with truth that we truly learn to see, feel, believe. No one can hope to experience everything in our lives; if you have something worth sharing, writing is the best way to do it.

We share through the beauty and power of language that which facts, numbers and dates just don't reach. Someone can read a medical review all about a child who had brain cancer, but that doesn't touch upon the human aspect of it. My poetry, for example, about my daughter's struggle with her brain cancer opens the window and lets the light in to her and our experience; you see, feel and strive to understand, thus experience. History is great; I am a big fan of the study of history, but it only provides information; it doesn't process the truth. Only you can do that. If one wanted to understand the war in Vietnam, for example, one could read historical accounts, but not really understand. To truly understand, you could read the poetry of Bruce Weigl, or the novels of Tim O'Brien and Martin Naparsteck. So if you really want to share who you are, free yourself to write. Writing helps to put experiences, life, into perspective and light; we can discover who we really are, where we've been and just maybe where we want to go. Art, the practice and study of it, opens our minds to the possibilities in life; we open our minds to finding substance and sense in our lives.

CHAPTER 8

OUR SPIRTS/OURSELVES

Going along with the power of poetry, the power of language, to help us understand who we are and maybe where we are going. I think of the words of poet, William Carlos Williams: "You may not find news in poetry, but if you look you may find ways to save lives." Something like that. I think he is saying that what is truly important isn't found within the pages of newspapers or magazines; that's just so much information, facts to ponder, but not to question. He is talking about the power of who we are, the essence of the human spirit and all we are capable of if we just give ourselves the chance. Often we become jaded or apathetic by the time we hit middle age; maybe that's the time to get back to where we should be.

Not too many years ago, Harvard, a good school, discovered that most doctors, MD's, don't reach their full potential until they are into their forties. They were encouraged to rethink the policy of only accepting people into medical school who still had years to practice; it was partly about cost, economics. In the past, medical schools rarely accepted students much beyond their early thirties. The study they did encouraged them to consider looking at accepting students into their forties. Why? The answer is that doctors usually become understanding human beings before they become doctors because of life's experiences after kicking around for a few extra years. So they came to the conclusion, why not admit people who have already experienced life, losses, joy and sorrow, and then train them. The end result is the same. The true loving, caring spirit of the person came before the training not after, as was the convention prior.

That's why when Oprah was on TV she was always talking about "Remembering the Spirit." It's because we are not giving enough attention to the essence of who we truly are; we forgot about the little baby we used to be who came into the world screaming and cold. We are more apt to be caught up in the person others have taught us to become other than who really should be. By the time we hit middle age we are so caught up in apathy and disappointment we have lost our vision. We only see what is before us, not what is still inside of us. We turn something on, because we don't like to be alone with ourselves, to keep us company. Look around; everyone is carrying cell phones in their hands, sending texts, blogging, disconnected from now.

For so many years I operated the same way. I would walk into the house and turn something on before I even took my coat off or said hello to the cat. I was so caught up in being distracted I never heard the caught say hello until I learned the importance of just being first. It means so much to our spirits to just be with ourselves, and enjoy our own company.

I think it really became clear to me when my daughter was in the hospital near death. It was almost a year after her brain surgery when she developed a terrible lung infection as a partial result from internal bleeding following stomach surgery meant to repair damage done while inserting a feeding tube to bolster nutrition. She contracted the lung disease following the emergency surgery. She was put into a induced coma in an effort to fight for her breath. It was so traumatic for all involved, especially her. She received the Last Rites of the Catholic Church more than once. Imagine being a parent standing at her bedside for that ritual and all we were taught that it meant. She missed Halloween, her favorite of all days; she missed Thanksgiving, Christmas, and New Year's Day; she was confirmed by the church when she was out as well. At one point the medical people were expecting her to have a numo thorax – a hole would pop in her lung and she would go into cardiac arrest. For a week, they would tell us every day that she would probably not make it through the night; but every night she did make it. She did have a numo, in fact it happened 14 times and she still held on with the strength of her will to live. Most of the time during her ordeal I felt alone and helpless and completely powerless.

At one point a Doctor John asked if we wanted to sign a DNR (do not resuscitate) if she was to go into cardiac arrest. A family member hesitated when the question was asked, and I fell to my knees, gabbed her ankles when she said, "let her go." I begged her not to even suggest that; I would not let my daughter go. She fought too long and hard; if she wasn't letting go; I wouldn't let her go. I was at a loss as to who I could count on, who would be with me through all of this? Yes family members and friends were there who tried to be comforting, but they couldn't feel what was in my heart. I remember that winter as especially cold and sunless. My days consisted of living in a fog of helplessness, sometimes drinking myself to sleep and hoping for someone to offer a hand to me during the day. I felt ignored by the in-laws as they seemed to maneuver for position, and I prayed for my daughter's life. Sometimes if there was a meeting with the medical people, they would give my family the wrong location; I still don't know why. And then my Mother died.

I was living in a studio apartment at the time. I had lived in bigger places since leaving my home, but wanted to try a place that had just enough room for me, Erin's cat, and my stuff. I figured, most of us spend the majority of our time at home operating within about four or five square feet anyway, so why did I need extra room? Well, I was wrong; living within limited confines sucks. It seemed coffin-like when I did have to go there and do whatever I had to do: sleep, drink, eat, think and be alone. It was dark, small; the walls seemed to be closing in on me especially at night. I found the space of the hospital to be less restrictive.

One morning I arrived at the hospital, as I always did, early. I was talking to some friends from work and visiting with Erin off and on as usual. One of the friends I was always happy to see was Bob. He was always a big comfort, someone who brought clarity and reason with him. My cousin Mary came into the parent's dungeon of a waiting room while I was speaking with Bob. I was surprised to see her because she had just been up the night before. She paced once, then twice, then stopped in front of me. She had tears in her eyes. "Your mother is dead" was all she could get out, and she said it quickly. I couldn't move, or think. I looked out the window at the brick wall across the courtyard. It seemed cloudy outside. I turned back to her, and I think I began crying. She explained to me that my Mother died during the night and one of the women from her building found her. My Mother was 74 years old and my daughter's best friend. I heaved a bit; a sour taste in my throat, and wondered how I would I tell Erin.

My Mother was very religious and tried to instill that into her kids. What she did a few days before she died didn't surprise me. As she aged the arthritis in her hips got worse; walking was quite painful for her. She used a cane. While my daughter was in the hospital, my mom would get up early every morning and begin her journey to see and be with Erin. It would take her forever to get there; she could only move so fast. She would ride the bus. She'd take one bus, transfer, take another and transfer and be there every day. She didn't want anyone to pick her up; she didn't want to impose; she didn't want anyone taking time away from being with her granddaughter. I recall going for coffee one morning and finding my Mother in a hospital wheelchair pulling herself along aided by the wall's hand rail on her way to see Erin. I insisted she let me push her to the room, but she refused saying, "I need to do this myself." I think it was that day she told us she had tried to phone the Pope the night before. She wanted to have the Pope pray for our girl. Surprise, she didn't get to speak to the Pope, but the priest she did talk with in Rome assured her that our girl would be prayed for

All of the family believe that my Mother went one better that night, the night she died. Rather than rely only on the Pope, she would solicit help from the main source of spiritual power, healing and love. My daughter, my Mother's best friend, graduated from high school on June 22, 2000, as am honors student. My Mother had died six years earlier and I still miss her, we all do. It was one of the most difficult things I ever had to do, telling my daughter that Grandma had died. It was after she finally came out of the coma that I told her.

She never mentioned my Mother after she woke up, never asked where she was, why she wasn't visiting her. This is a girl who refused to go for brain surgery the day after the tumor was discovered until her Grandma was there to give her a kiss. One day, about two weeks after she woke up she was crying as she lay in the bed hooked up to monitors and IV's. She didn't often display the pain she was feeling, the fear that must have always been with her; she didn't want to worry or upset the rest of us. I asked her what was wrong? At first, not unlike her, she was reluctant to share what was bothering her. She finally said, after some prodding, through tears, "Grandma doesn't love me anymore. That's when I told her that her grandmother loved her so much she had to go and speak with God directly to keep you here with all of us who need you so much. My daughter wasn't dumb; she knew what I was saying.

I will never forget the sound that came from deep inside of her when I told her her best friend was dead. I don't know where that sound came from, where that deep part of sorrow dwells within all of us, what deep, loving part of the soul, the spirit unleashed that wail of grief and loss. I do know that never have I heard, or probably will ever hear again, such a complete and true sound of agony and pain; at that moment I believe I heard the very real sound of the agony of human suffering. She mourned and cried and asked questions, and all but forgot about what she was going through because she missed her Grandma so, so much. Once again, my daughter gave birth to me; once again she opened my eyes and sent me wailing into the world. It's moments like this that define who we are and who we need to become: embrace them.

Following Erin's brain surgery, she had to undergo a series of tests to ensure the cancer had not violated other areas of her tiny body. One of these tests was a bone marrow test. We were told it would not be a pleasant experience; medical people can be so subtle when it comes to relating issues of pain. The oncologist was to insert a probe deep within her hip to extract a marrow sample for testing. All they could really do by way of pain relief was to numb the skin where the probe would be inserted. I suppose they try and avoid general anesthesia when possible. The process itself, we were told, would be extremely painful for Erin. Only one of the parents could remain in the room because of space limitations and the challenge of the test itself. Erin chose me. I never told her, but that moment was a revelation to me as a dad, a moment of joy, sorrow and triumph. This child, my child wanted me to be with her. She also knew how upset her mom could become. They had the rest of the family wait in a room a distance down the hall. I learned later that it was because children would often scream in such agony loved ones would lose it.

I positioned myself near Erin's head as the test began. I spoke to her softly telling of my deep love for her. The room was as large as a small bedroom with one window behind my daughter; it was a cloudy day. The walls were a pale, off white, with just the exam table, equipment cart and a single chair on which I sat. I asked her, where she would like to be if she could be anyplace else? She thought a moment, closed her eyes, started to speak but stopped. I kissed her forehead. Finally she said, "Oz." She loved that movie, almost as much as she loved "Willy Wonka and the Chocolate Factory" later in life. I remember wishing I could whisk her away to OZ right then.

As the procedure began, we talked about the wonderful land of Oz, and the magic and promise it offered. She liked the Munchkins. I could detect from the corner of my eye the doctor beginning the test. I could see the manipulation, the thrusting and digging he had to do to extract the sample. The medical people were active and focused; one doctor and two nurses. I could only imagine the pain she was experiencing as the test progressed; they seemed aggressive in their efforts. Erin was on her stomach; I had my right hand on her back and my left hand holding her head, stroking her hair; it was so soft and fine. She didn't cry, she didn't call out insisting they stop. The only telling detail she was in pain was a tiny tear on her cheek and the squeeze of my hand I had moved from her back to hold her left hand under the sheet. She was still, as they requested, even for the most intense part of the procedure. It seemed to go on forever as I whispered in her ear about Dorothy and Toto and how all she wanted to do was just go home. At one point, I attempted to sing, "Somewhere over the Rainbow." I wasn't sure, but I think I saw one side of her mouth curl into a little smile. She would always put her little hand over my mouth when I tried to sing, even when she was little, little. Finally they finished. And when I looked their way and thought I detected Erin tapping her heals together moving under the sheet.

It was all over. The doctor and nurses applauded; I cried. The medical people marveled at her strength and courage. All three agreed, they couldn't remember a child before Erin go through such a procedure as brave. Later I asked Erin why she didn't cry; it must have hurt so much? I was so amazed at her courage, her ability to deal with what must have been so terribly painful. Yes, she told me, it did hurt a lot, but she didn't want to cry or scream even though it might have helped. She said she didn't want to worry or upset me and Oz helped. How do you respond when your 11-year-old is more worried about you than the pain she's enduring? I kissed her and helped her put her slippers on. The doctor slapped me on the back and said, "You two make a great team." I told him I knew it. We were all crying softly, Erin's mom, brothers and me, as we wheeled her back to her room. The spirit of this child both comforted me and confused me.

When my cousin told me my Mother had died, I just sat in the waiting room softly sobbing. One of the pediatric doctors, young, tall with dark hair came into the room. I didn't know him; he wasn't working with Erin; I had just seen him around the ward. He sat down on the dark blue, fake leather couch and put his arm around my shoulders. His grip around me was deliberate when he said, "Everything will be all right." For some reason, some how I believed him. I experienced a moment, just a moment, of calm, peace. Later that day I went looking for him to thank him for his kindness. I checked the ward, the nurses' station, even went down to the cafeteria to look for him. I couldn't find him anywhere. I asked some of the doctors and nurses who he was, where I might find him; I didn't explain. Maybe my description was faulty; no one could help me; no one seemed to know who I was talking about. I was almost positive I had seen him in the past, but at that moment wasn't really sure. Was I imagining it all? No, my cousin told me, he was there; he hugged and said something she didn't hear. I never did see him again for the remaining months Erin was in the hospital that time. I realized, acknowledged that I was alive and so was Erin.

It wasn't long after my Mother's death that I believe I felt something leave inside of me and make room for something else. So much had happened, so many assaults on the senses and the heart had ushered a change of sorts; I just felt different or the beginning of something different and new.

It was gradual as time progressed, but it was sure and true. Something inside of me seemed to be waking up. I didn't and still don't know what to call it; it just was. Part of what I felt was realizing that I needed to find comfort within myself, to just be and look beyond all the superficial crap that doesn't matter and acknowledge what is really important. like love and empathy and compassion and understanding.

Sometimes after that when things would be oppressive in the hospital for one reason or another. I would just go off and be by myself to think and try and figure things out. I would spend time in that dark waiting room when no one else was there, turn the sound down on the TV and just sit. Sometimes I would lay down on that terrible couch and doze off and dream. I didn't go home to have a drink, to get a break, to be away. I was learning to be away within myself. I began to stop beating myself up about things I had no control over. I still worried and cried and felt and alone, but it was different, not as hopelessly intense.

One of the problems I began to develop in middle age that was less pronounced when I was younger was to worry about things I would have considered silly when I was younger. Okay, I have a meeting at work tomorrow, a review, so I would spend the entire evening worrying about it. Hell, I might have a dentist appointment in a month, and when we grew up dentist appointments were hell, might as well start worrying about it now, so by the time it gets here I cancel it, or just don't show up because I've been thinking about it too damn much and convinced myself to be afraid. That can be an incredible waste of time and mind occupation. That goes back to the real power of the imagination; we never totally lose that ability to sense pain at the dentist or ghosts in the closet. That's just not productive or healthy.

We have to stop waking up in the morning and worrying about everything we have to accomplish during the day even before we get out of the shower and eat a pop tart. Have some faith in your abilities; you've made it to middle age;

you must have some idea what the hell you're doing. If you need to think in the shower, think about the joy that exists in your life, or the joy that could exist in your life if you were to just get a bit closer to the person that is truly who you are. Spend some time staring out of the window looking at the birds, watching people and wondering who they are, what they looked like when they were younger, who they love, who loves them. Learn to really see people; learn to really see birds. Birds are cool even if they do dump on our cars and picnic tables. I remember in AIT (advanced individual training) in the Army, we were in morning formation when a seagull took a big dump on the captain and the top sergeant had to wipe it off. It made for a good day for us. Birds seem to get along, mostly. The best thing about birds is that they can fly and don't care if we watch them. No matter what time my first class is in the morning, I always get into work at least an hour early. I enjoy looking out at the sky watching the birds, planes descending to the nearby airport, the shape of the clouds. I try to relax before the day begins and BE, and not worry, and think about the air passing in and out of my lungs and the birds and sky and my family and the beauty that's always there if we would just take time to see it and be present.

TWO WORLDS

I guess finding that spirit within ourselves is a lot about paying attention. That's not always an easy thing to do considering we are rarely required to do it. It's about paying attention to the world around us and the world, spirit within each of us. It's about the duality of nature and spirit. And how, in order to find joy and peace in our lives, we should always live in both worlds, on the river, in the middle. Always remember, perception is reality. Check out some Eastern Philosophy.

For most of us, the world of nature, the physical world is very familiar and comfortable for us to exist in; it's what we know, see and feel. But it's not who we are; it's what we perceive. That's only part of what life is about; but we concentrate so much on the material we often end up unhappy. I'm not even sure what the word, "happy" means; it's so vague and ambiguous and ephemeral. If you drink a few beers you might feel happy, but that is fleeting. Attend a child's event, dance, baseball game, a play and you'll feel proud; and pride, memory lasts forever. We're taught in our culture to live with the material manifestations of existence; we react only to the five senses and the payback we receive. We see, we want, we hear; but we don't really listen. We taste, like, don't like; we smell, we shower; we make promises we don't keep. We are encouraged to pursue the material things life offers, the stuff of the material world, and we attach these things of substance to happiness, or at least we believe that is what joy is. But joy isn't without. It's within; it's in the heart, the soul, the memory of my children's laughter.

We want the house, the car, the ipod, the smart phone, the clothes, the jewelry. We want all of those things that will mean nothing when we are on our death beds. Who is going to want to clutch their bank statements when he's dying; no one. We'll want the touch of a loved one; the kiss of a child. There's nothing wrong with wanting a new care, the look, the smell; the sense of self entitlement it might provide; but how long does it last? Sure, you take care of it because it's an investment. But eventually the joy is fleeting; it becomes something just to get you from here to there and maintain. We ignore our feelings because middle aged men aren't supposed to feel, or at least how our feelings. We ignore who we are and cultivate what others, we think, see us as. Why? We too often allow our external reality to shape our inner vision of ourselves; it should be the other way around. It's our internal vision of who we are, the desire to love and learn that should shape how we live our lives and the world we live in. Okay, so we lost touch with that child in us, that imagination that gave us joy, that spirit that lives within each and every one of us; but it's still there, waiting to be reawakened.

CHAPTER 9

INNER VISION

How and when did we come to a sense of ourselves? What do we hope and dream for our lives; do we even know where the dreams began? As young men we often emulated the males who just happen to be the closest to us. How else would we learn how to become men unless it was through observation? Maybe the men we learned to be forty or so years ago no longer fit in today's world. Maybe we had poor role models to emulate; or just maybe, if you are anything like me, we had no role models in our lives. So what did we learn?

Many of us even with close male figures in our lives often learned to become men from all of the wrong sources. Dad, if he was around, worked so damn much we never got to see him or learn anything of significance about him. He'd be that guy who would come home grumpy after work because he never reached his potential, lost sight of his inner vision, and sat comatose in front of the TV until we children disappeared upstairs. He would usually be too damn busy on the weekends taking care of all the business he was too tired to take care of during the week. The last thing we wanted to do was to disturb him and ask him to throw us the ball, or just sit down and talk. For many of us middle agers, Dad was just a stranger we saw once in awhile who paid the bills and got up with us on Christmas morning. So, we learned from watching TV, hanging out with our friends who didn't know anymore about becoming a man than we did, and we ended up all screwed up and confused looking for some kind of direction and understanding of who we were supposed to be.

Should I be like my father, many of us may have asked ourselves, at least secretly. Maybe we didn't want to be like our fathers, or be what they seemed to be. I'm not sure young men often imitate their fathers, at least professionally, from nature or nurture. Does a policeman's son become a policeman because of his father's influence, or because he is genetically predisposed to have the same interests and desires? It's a tough question. My father, even though he wasn't around for me growing up, was a machinist of sorts most of his life. If I had to make a list of potential career choices when I was younger, anything having to do with mechanics or machinery wouldn't have even found its way onto my list. I never really knew what I wanted to be; being me seemed like a good idea, but I was never quite sure who that was or what it meant. After more than a couple different careers, I ended up as a college professor. Go figure. My oldest son just completed his BA in English and is considering going on because he thinks he would like to teach college. Now does that mean our shared genes have influenced him, or my example is steering him in that direction? I never encouraged him into the field; I wanted him to find his own way. Well I suppose we should leave that to the scientists to ponder and just take a look at how we came to be whatever it is we are and maybe, just maybe, why. I believe the key point here is that it is never too late to become what we should have been. But what should we have been?

LIFE'S STAGES

FIRST STAGE

Maybe if we take a look at the three basic stages of life, we might start to get some insight into what we are all about, and how we came to be us. The first stage of life is all about learning the basics. We learn most from our parents, or whoever raises us and tries to guide us. We human beings come into this world pretty helpless. If we didn't have anyone taking care of us we would just lay around making noises and most probably developing a complex requiring years of therapy. But luckily we all have someone who takes on the responsibility of our initial care, usually Mom. Moms are great people to have around when you're helpless; for some of us that may last a bit longer. Moms feed us, clean us up, talk to us, give great hugs and kisses, and sing even if they can't. We soon learn to recognize them and look forward to what they give us. We are learning to count on someone for care, and love. But we also learn so much more during this very important early stage of growth and discovery.

It's all carefully calculated to help us reach a potential and goal so we can leave their house and go off on our own to find happiness. Even before we venture off to school, we learn how to communicate, and share, and stay safe, and not slobber and pee in corners. We learn what it will take to survive when we go off to school and interact with people other than our family members who have to treat us somewhat reasonably because we are related. It's not always an easy task to prepare a child for the cruel world of school, and all the dangers it might present. We learn there are mean people in the world, even little mean people. We realize we are not the center of the universe; that's one hell of a shock for many of us. We are thrust into having to learn how to get along and slowly become productive members of society. As we all know, it takes a long time. In grammar school we learn many of the basics required as we progress from grade to grade. We are being prepared for the next step in the process. And all the time we are being influenced by all kinds of people and experiences that we can't even begin to decipher and make sense of. So it all gets filed away to eventually add up to our personalities and character.

It's during this step when we begin to form friendships based on many factors, including what we night have in common. This is when we begin to consider how others might see us and regard who we think we are. We may even begin to alter our behavior just a bit to please others. Already we are beginning to disregard who we are just to fit in. Not that there is anything wrong with fitting in; it's great to fit in, but at what expense is the question. We are also getting ready for high school where all types of interesting things begin to happen to us.

In high school we continue to build upon everything that came before, including academics, and socializing with our peers, and answering to authority. This is all the stuff we'll need to have practiced before we enter the big world of adulthood, and all the responsibility that goes along with it. Things can really begin to get tough in high school. However we may see ourselves, this is where we establish, or begin to, our place within the various classes we seem to manufacture. High school is where there seems to be lots of competition to gain some sort of status and earn our place.

Our internal vision of ourselves has been so influenced by outside forces by high school, that often we have lost total touch with who we truly are. We are always putting on a face when we walk out of the door in the morning to meet the perceived expectations of others. We believe, really believe, it is so important to wear the right clothes, have the right hair, drive the right car, and be all that popularity requires. This is all external stuff that really has no value whatsoever, and we know it, but still we buy into it. My first car was a 1962 Chevy Corvair that I bought when I was in tenth grade for $250. I had a before school job where I served coffee and doughnuts to Kodak workers from 5 A.M. to 7:30 A.M. every morning. I paid my own insurance, and basically my own way. It was important for me to have a car; what 16-year-old boy doesn't want a car? In fact, I had my car even before I had my driver's license. I had little patience at that age; I needed and wanted everything immediately. After having this car for almost a year, I decided I needed a better one, one with more prestige. I really thought my friends thought less of me because my car was less than impressive. So I went out and got a loan and bought a 1967 Pontiac Tempest with a 326 engine. The engine was very important for some reason. So here I was 16 years old and in debt because of appearance and prestige when in fact the Corvair was just as good transportation as anything else; except of course Ralph Nader said it was unsafe at any speed. Hell, I was 16, who gave a shit. I didn't have the car three weeks when a woman ran a stop sign and totaled my prestigious car. When the insurance company settled, my Mother made me pay off the loan and start walking again. I did and figured my status went with my car. Stupid, right? Of course it was, but that's the way we thought at that age; and that's the way young people still think. Hey, I was just as intelligent and good looking without the car, but I believed I had become all but invisible. I was defining myself by a possession.

Actually I believe high school's main intent and value is to keep teenagers off the streets as long as possible, and hope most mature enough to be marginally productive. But those years are also a time for us to experience new things that will continue to give us some experience in what it might be like to be all grown up and responsible. We often experience the work force for the first time in high school. We learn what it's like to have a job, all be it in the service industry for most of us. We quickly figure out that in order to get paid, we need to show up at work and do whatever it is they are paying us for a certain amount of time, and a certain number of days a week. It's not always easy at that age, especially considering that most of us are still living with our parents.

I have had jobs as short as three hours when I was in high school. One particular short stint in the labor force was at a convenience store. The first hour wasn't too bad, but the second and third really got to me. I couldn't stand waiting on sticky little kids with their pennies and nickels and snotty noses. I swore that the next kid that asked me for popcorn would be my last. Sure enough, a kid wanted popcorn and I quit. So back to the street corner I went to hang out with my other unemployed friends doing absolutely nothing but being cool; so we thought.

High school also offers us the opportunity to begin to form intimate relationships with members of the opposite sex, or not, and bond. Having a girlfriend, the right girlfriend in high school was an important thing for me to do. There were other reasons I wanted a girlfriend, but that rarely came to anything. I don't know about the rest of you guys, but getting a girl to have sex with me was about as far from happening as my becoming an accountant. But did we ever try. Although there was this girl who lived across the street from me when I was 16 who did make my dreams come true if only for a little while. But I digress. The first real girlfriend I had in high school was named was Marilyn. I was in tenth grade and I had been out drinking beer with my friends prior to stopping at the local dance, one of which was happening every Friday night someplace in my neighborhood. I knew her from school; even knew her well enough to say hello to. So when I saw her at the dance, I asked her to dance; something I know I wouldn't have done sober. So we danced the night away, and when the dance was over I asked her if I could walk her home. My God she said yes; and I did. Half way to her house (had I known how far it was I wouldn't have asked in the first place). I asked her if she would go out with me. My God she said yes. Wow, I had me a real live girlfriend. So for the next month I would walk her to class and sit on her living room couch while her mother stared at me, and give her kisses good-bye. I remember hoping marriage had more to offer. We would talk on the phone about nothing, and write notes about nothing at school. I do recall trying to stick my hand up her shirt once, but almost lost it; that message was clear. But she was pretty and popular, which was really important to whatever image I thought I had. It wasn't too long after we started going out that she broke my heart. I was kind of tired of the whole thing; and besides, I was missing all of the wonderful times my friends were having without me. We were at yet another dance when a classmate, a real cool guy, asked her to dance. She declined, shooting a regretful glance my way. Next thing I knew she disappeared with mister hot shot, and I was left to friend my friends. It wasn't hard; they were on the corner smoking and spitting. I did feel a bit inadequate; I had lost a girlfriend and worried about what people would think of me. Deep down I really didn't care, but like many of us at that age I was no longer working from within; I was working from without.

I think high school is when it really becomes solidified for us not to like school. It wasn't terribly cool to be smart, do well, or show respect to the teachers. Why? How the hell do I know? I think it was stupid, so were we at that age. I used to pride myself on not ever bringing a book home in all four years. When my grade report would come home, my Mother would just shake her head reading it. I usually would receive an E, failing each marking period in almost every class. The way I got through high school was to ace the regents finals all the time. (Regents was the equivalent of honors). That was when you could pass the regents and pass the course. The night before the finals, I would read the text books from cover to cover. I suppose that does show I did have potential, but what would my friends have thought. Now all I can say is, who gives a shit. But that's not what I felt then. I was not operating from within, I was operating from all of those external ideas I thought were important. By the time we finish high school we have pretty much lost whatever internal vision we had of ourselves and replaced it with society's definition of who we were supposed to be and become.

For many of us high school is the culmination of a lot of training and exposure to what others have done before us. So that means we are supposed to follow their paths, which is ridiculous when you think about it. We all need to find our own paths in life, not follow in the steps of people who are not us. But we do anyway and get a job, or go to college to specialize in whatever we are going to do for the next forty or so years. College is just like high school except it's easier to get beer. No, not really. College, for the right reasons, is more important than anything else we've done in our lives up to this point.

In all reality, college is the part of this first stage of life that should be continued throughout the rest of our lives. No, we need not attend college eternally, although it's not a bad idea. We need to continue pursuing what college encourages us to find; and that's knowledge. We should never end our quest for knowledge; it is the pursuit of knowledge that keeps the mind young and always open to new ideas and experiences. This is the only true way we can expand our intellects and experience balanced growth in body mind and spirit. But unfortunately in our society we compartmentalize our lives to suit predetermined notions and often convoluted dictates of others.

We are only supposed to follow the path of education, formally speaking anyway, for a prescribed amount of time. After that, we are to jump into the workforce and become a productive member of society; whatever the hell that means. So in reality, and generally in practice, the first stage of life is really all about preparation for the second stage of life. We spend the first 18 to 20+ years of our lives acquiring the knowledge necessary for us to have a comfortable and happy second stage. We choose a career path, or find one that we hope will not only bring us financial security, but also professional fulfillment. But unfortunately it doesn't always work out that way; one doesn't necessarily guarantee the other. I'm sure we all know more than a few people who make a decent living, but are not particularly happy in what they are doing. Somewhere during the first stage of life we bought into the idea that money could purchase a certain amount of happiness. Think about how ridiculous that notion is; and now that we are in middle age we have the experience to give that convoluted idea some serious thought.

When I think about the most joyous moments of my life, money does not factor in at all. Always go back to the joy in your life; that's where true happiness exists. Make a list of the most joyous moments in your life; and then go to what those moments were made of; go to what lead you to those moments. Remember Christmas mornings when you were a kid; better yet, remember the anticipation of Christmas mornings. It wasn't really about the gifts; it was about the surprise, the joy of waiting to discover the unknown and the new. It was about bright lights and colors and smells and voices and family togetherness. It was all about being safe and truly loved and cherished.

When I think about the joyous moments in my life I think about walking across the tarmac at the airport after spending almost two years in the Army, and seeing three people waiting for me through the glass. It was that moment that I came home for; it was that moment that defined my life up to that point. And that moment was free; a memory I wouldn't sell for a million dollars. The truly joyous moments in our lives are those memories no one would sell for a million dollars. My four-year-old son winning a foot race at a Fourth of July festival is such a moment. My other son going to the first birthday party away from his family at a friend's house. He was five and had to be talked into it. I so much just wanted to turn the car around and bring him home, but I knew how important it was for him to walk into that house and let go of my hand. And he did it; and I cried on the way home. That's what life, truly living, is really all about.

What did it cost me to comb my daughter's long hair to get ready for school in the morning? It cost nothing, but gave me the joy of gentleness and trust. I have lived a lifetime in a day for only the cost of twelve night crawlers when I took my kids fishing. For the cost of those worms, I heard "Dad" all day long. I experienced and reveled in the joy and accomplishments of their smiles, and even their arguing. And that joy will last me forever and a day. I have a colleague who had a picnic at his house for our department a number of years ago when my kids were much younger; before my daughter got sick. To this day, he still reminds me of how my three children went canoeing on his pond and made the noise of life. That's his as well as my fondest memory of that day. That cost me a few dollars in gas to get to his house. But I will remember and cherish that more than anything I ever purchased with a dollar. So we spend the first stage of our lives getting ready for the second with misdirected ideas about what we are supposed to pursue and accomplish as productive adults. But enter the second stage we do, and we struggle to make our way as best we can.

SECOND STAGE

For most of us, the second stage of life is probably the longest. The part where we are suppose to spend the first part of our lives acquiring knowledge, the second stage offers us the opportunity to acquire experience and make that knowledge pay off. These are the two primary paths we follow in life: the path of the acquisition of knowledge, and the path of the acquisition of experience. Unfortunately in our culture, we follow these two paths separately. The duality of our beings, who we truly are, really dictates that we follow these two paths simultaneously, for it is with the combination of knowledge and experience that true wisdom is born. But many of us, particularly in middle age, reject this notion and spend a good portion of the second stage of our lives only acquiring experience based on material acquisition. What's up with that?

When we spend too much time working to make the money to buy the things we never really needed in the first place, we lose touch with who we are; we lose touch with our spirits. Money is like the time thing: we are saving up as much as we can and we don't even know for sure what we want to do with it. We get all caught up in our careers, and don't even know our children, or our wives until we, or they, are calling a lawyer because somebody is tired of living with a stranger. We don't know anybody anymore, especially ourselves. But the cars are in the driveway, and the pool is in the yard and the big screen TV is our closest friend. What's the point? I know because I was kind of there. I was all caught up in the Me of life, and the needs I had, and the fact that I had little patience with those who weren't being me. I screwed up and lost sight of what really mattered. But even a screw up can be positive if we learn from it, and grow as human beings. My love for the people in my life is in tact, and nothing will ever get in the way of that again. It's never, ever too late to learn and revive the sense of yourself and your spirit.

Even though the kids' Mom and I are not together anymore, she will always be an important part of who I am because she was an important part of who I was. We all buy into the requirements of the second stage of life. We move on the path of getting a job, getting married, having kids, buying everything we can possibly cram into our various cramming places. But then, for some of us, it all falls apart; it falls apart because we lost sight of the joy and how to make that joy happen. We got too damn busy trying to achieve what everyone expected of us, but had little to do with paying attention to our spirits and knowledge and growth. This past Mother's Day I purchased the kids' Mom a diamond bracelet. I recall telling one of my colleagues about the gift I was going to give Toniann on Mother's day, and she was a bit surprised that I was giving such a nice gift to someone I was no longer sharing a life with. At first I explained that we would always be sharing our lives because we share three beautiful children. I went on to explain my reasoning behind the gift I chose to give. Sure I could have given her a fruit basket, or hankies, or bath soaps; kind of like the stuff we gave the Nuns for Christmas; the thought that counts kind of thing. But those kind of gifts wouldn't truly say what I wanted to convey.

I wanted her to know how grateful I was; how much I truly appreciated her as the kids' Mother. I wanted to know I understood she was the one to get the kids up in the morning and get them off to school after I left the house. I wanted her to know that I knew she was the one who stayed up with them at night when they were sick. I wanted to thank her for being there to listen to their troubles and complaints. I wanted to thank her for feeding them, washing their clothes, laughing at their silly jokes, hanging their drawings on the frig, and every moment I wasn't there to help. I wanted to thank her for every single moment I envy and regret not having. I wanted to let her know I knew, and would always know what she went through and did for our children. And like I signed the card: "To a wonderful Mother, from a grateful father." I wanted her to know she was more than appreciated. I kind of thought a diamond bracelet was just a small way to let her know how I felt, and always will. "Thank you, Toniann." My spirit finally woke up.

It is often all of these attitudes that we developed during the first stage of life that guide us through the second. The work ethic is important; it feeds us, shelters and clothes us. We usually believe in everything the Declaration of Independence gave us, especially our own pursuit of happiness. But we allow, even encourage, too many outside influences to guide us through life. We have lost sight of the true bliss that was ours before we discovered what we presume others admire us for. Think about the people you really admire. Does it have anything to do with the kind of car they drive, or how big their house is? Probably not. You probably admire people you know for their kindness, their ability to communicate, maybe their own sense of their spirit.

So we find ourselves living in two worlds; the duality of nature and spirit; the paths of knowledge and experience; but we don't always live in these two worlds simultaneously, and often fail to discover the wisdom that will truly make us whole, spiritual human beings who aren't afraid to allow our internal selves to shine through and light the darkness that exists in the external world. The second stage of life should really be about giving, not acquiring material possessions that will be forgotten long before the smile of a child, the laughter of a friend. There are so many ways to get reacquainted with your internal, spiritual self. The material things in life are so fleeting; they all eventually end up in the land fill. It's the memories we hold in our hearts that will last forever. I believe we are here on this planet for two reasons: to love and to learn. The love we give will always equal the love we receive. The most important things that we can give to ourselves is love, empathy and compassion, and those are the most important gifts we can give to our children. At the end of it all, the most important things we should be remembered for, have inscribed on our tombstones, could be: he lived, he loved, he laughed, he cried, he died.

It's important in middle age to get back in touch, and find new life in our internal selves and be the person we were always meant to be until the second stage of life got in our way and confused our vision and goals. You don't have to wait until the third stage of life to put it all together. Be practical and allow your heart to guide and speak for you a bit more than in the past. Act on an impulse to be nice. Open who you are, your heart, to others and it will all come back to you.

Sometimes getting back in touch with our spirits, our internal selves is as simple as just thinking and reacting differently than we are used to. What helps me to calm down and relax is accepting the fact that everything happens for a reason. We don't always learn what the reason is, at least not right away, but stuff happens for a reason. I believe we need to experience whatever life throws at us for us to become what we need to become when we need to be there for others as well as ourselves. It's all about growth and shedding negative feelings and attitudes.

Think about how you react when you catch a red light and you are in a hurry to get someplace. You probably get a little tense, maybe even angry at the light, or your luck. What purpose does that serve? None at all. The light will change, and you will arrive at your destination one or two minutes later. Maybe you weren't supposed to get through that light. The point is that we just don't know. Accept fate, and accept your place in the moment that belongs to you and you alone. When you are challenged, accept the challenge to learn and grow. It doesn't mean you have to like it, but it is your challenge and your life: deal with it.

One of the most difficult challenges in my life was when my daughter was diagnosed with a brain tumor. I asked myself over and over again, why her? She was the most loving and caring and beautiful child that God had ever created. The answer is there is no answer. Why she had to have brain cancer is a question that has no immediate discernible answer, but that doesn't mean it didn't happen for a reason. It could have happened for hundreds of reasons; all of them unfair of course. This challenge she faced brought people together who never would have shared time in their lives before. This challenge of hers had all kinds of people praying for her, even people who didn't believe in God prayed for her. Her challenge changed me, and I am sure many others, for the rest of my life. I finally accepted something I had probably suspected prior to her challenge, that the most important thing in life, that which takes precedent over everything else, is very simply LOVE. Sometimes I joke with my students, and tell them I know the meaning of life; why we're all here. But I really believe I do know, but it is up to each individual to discover and accept them on their own. It is up to each person to look into themselves and find the truth and accept the truth. The meaning of life, of course, is To Love; and the reason we are all here, is To Learn. I don't mean to learn in the academic sense; I mean to learn and grow in the spiritual sense...however you want to define that. Maybe it's just as simple as learning to be better people.

There are so many opportunities to be kind to people each and every day of our lives. Once I swiped my grocery discount card for the guy in line in front of me because he didn't have one. It didn't take a lot of effort, but I touched his life and will probably never see him again. No big deal, but the little things do add up. Just for the record, I am not a big fan of those grocery discount cards everyone seems to be carrying on their key chains today. I found mine in the parking lot because I don't want some organization somewhere keeping track of what I buy. I just don't want to get tons of coupons for cat food, beer, and cheese whiz: I mean, who does? Be kind to strangers; smile, open a door for someone and say hello.

I think work can be one of the most difficult places for many of us to practice random acts of kindness for a lot of reasons. And remember, things happen for a reason; you need to become who you need to become in order to deal with what life throws your way. Step up to the next level spiritually and you'll be amazed at how much better you feel, and how much better people feel being around you. Accept the fact that people can't help being who they are; and whatever their problems might happen to be, they are not your issues. It's when we begin to take things too personally that we fall into the trap of agonizing over that which we can't do a damn thing about in the first place.

When I was in the Army, my Mother gave me some really good advice that I call upon anytime I am going through something unpleasant. I remember bitching about having to go overseas, missing my girlfriend, missing out on all of the good times my friends would be having. She said, "You're going to be not going through this a lot longer than you're going to be going through it." I guess she was kind of telling me, all things, especially the bad, come to an end. She also told me that all I would go through would give me good experience; to consider it all an adventure. At first I didn't believe her. I still missed my girlfriend. I remember going to the mail room hoping from a letter from her and there wouldn't be one. I would go the next day and still there wasn't a letter from the girl I loved so much; and the next day; and the next. After almost a week without a letter I began to envision things, make up scenarios regarding my girlfriend. I saw her at drive-ins with other boys, at movies; I even saw her give her first kiss to her new boyfriend now that she had decided to dump me. I was devastated; I wanted to go AWOL and go home to try and talk her out of leaving me, a lonely soldier so far from home. Then I went to the mail room, and there were seven letters from her. That's the mail service for you. She still loved me and waited for me; although she didn't wait for the person she said good-bye to.

It was the same with my friends. We all know how important friends are to us as teenagers. I was really concerned that my friends would deliberately have fun without me there; I was even angry with them. I remember sitting in the bar we had been going to since we were 16 years old the night before I was to report to go away for basic training. Hell I grew up with these guys and couldn't imagine being away from them for two years. Even though I was in the beginning of my second stage in life, although I have jumped back and forth many times, and eventually found out how to follow both paths at once, the last thing I was concerned with was growth and the acquisition of experience. I wanted to hang around with my lazy, goalless friends. So I said goodbye to them and walked out of the bar with the image of the half dozen or so of them sitting at their self-assigned bar stools. For the sake of brevity here, two years later I came home, went to the bar, and found all of my friends sitting in about the same spots they were when I left two years prior. So much for missing the good times. What I didn't miss was an experience that turned out to be one of the most profound experiences of my life; as many veterans will agree. I suppose, that suggests that things are never what they seem; they are usually what we make them. The point is to give yourself credit; you can handle whatever life throws at you and come out of it a much better person.

During this second stage of life, we tend to concentrate far too much of our energies on the job and making money and dealing with all that goes with those things. But when all is said and done, how we paid the bills has little consequence regarding how we might be remembered in the end and beyond. When I was a technical writer in industry, one of my many assignments was to put together a retirement pamphlet for an outgoing VP. They also wanted a catchy saying to be included, an original catchy saying. So I came up with about a dozen and the one they chose went something like this: "A man is truly successful when he is remembered more for his efforts than he is for his accomplishments." I still don't know what that means, but they liked it and used it. But it does say something about how we live our lives, and the importance of making the most of each moment and not spend too much time planning for the future. Like the philosopher said, "we make plans and God laughs."

The experience we are acquiring during the second stage of life does not have to consist only of what is derived from work and the mundane moments of life that seem so abundant. The truly important experience we should be pursuing should revolve around the important things in life. Spending time with the people you care about is the most valuable thing you can do in middle age, even if work has to suffer. Get up Saturday morning and put Mozart on the CD player, read to your children no matter how old they are. Bring your kids to a movie. Once I brought my 18-year-old daughter to a movie on a Saturday afternoon. We had popcorn and whispered to each other about the film as it was playing, and just had a really great time together. Enjoy the company of your children; get to know them again. Enjoy the company of your partner; get to know her again. It's never too late; just like it's never too late to get that fat, out of shape body into shape. Make the second stage of life just as productive as the first. Where in the first you prepared yourself for life, prepare yourself for every day now, grow and stretch in every way. Follow the two paths at the same time and enter into the third stage of life with contentment and grace.

THIRD STAGE
Ideally the first stage of life, the acquisition of knowledge, combined with the second stage of life, the acquisition of experience, should lead to the realization of wisdom. This is all cultural stuff when you really give it some thought. We do have our lives broken into three stages, particularly in Western Culture. In order to function the way we think we are supposed to, like many who have come and gone before us, we need clearly defined beginnings and endings. We need to know when something is over, and when something is beginning, and unfortunately we don't always have control over those issues in our lives. It's like when I was laid off from Eastman Kodak Company over fifteen years ago after five years of faithful service. I have to admit it was the first solid, promising job I had up to that point in my life. I was a technical writer, and after only two years with the company I was promoted to team leader. I didn't particularly like the regimentation of industry, but I had the opportunity to be somewhat creative and I liked that; hell, I thought it was great they were paying me what they were paying me. But then came the layoffs; last hired first fired was their philosophy. What they seemed to fail to take into account is that they

were getting rid of a lot of good employees and keeping those who were just kind of sliding through their jobs; they had learned the ins and outs and how to get away with doing as little as possible. But they got rid of me and about 30,000 other people over the next few years. I wasn't alone, but I felt alone. That ended; that door closed, and I didn't know what I was going to do.

Anybody who has lost a decent job knows what thoughts and fears crop up: will I get another job? Will I be able to pay my bills? Will I be able to take care of my family? It wasn't easy; I wasn't prepared for that abrupt of an ending. We never are; but I survived. Today I believe it was the best thing to happen to me professionally speaking. Because they laid me off I found my way into teaching; the best, most fulfilling job in the world as far as I'm concerned. So I thank Kodak for giving me the opportunity to start all over again. Another door opened for me and my family.

It's when things end with little or no warning that we panic; we haven't been afforded the time to plan for the next step. But life isn't always like that because we try and make plans and be sure of what is happening to us. That's why we like the fact our lives are about the stages and all that they entail. We go to school; we go to work and have a family; we retire and die. That's what the third stage of life is all about; it's about retirement, and most importantly it is about reflection, at least it should be. After putting forty some odd years into the work force we expect to be able to sit back, relax and do what we want in our golden years. But how often do people get to their golden years and find they have nothing to do. At least they feel they have nothing to offer in a productive sense anymore.

That's not to say that when people retire they all sit around and just wait to die. Most people who are lucky enough to have had a career that paid well for more than a few years probably plan quite extensively for their retirement. The retirement years may be many, they may not be; we never know. But thanks to a large degree to Franklin Roosevelt we can even approximate the age we will retire and relax, and reflect. These are the years where wisdom should truly be ours, but it doesn't always work out that way. We spend far too many years concentrating too much on the acquisition of stuff and not enough time paying attention to our inner selves, our spiritual beings. Without the combination of always fostering both the internal and external selves, we lose sight of who we are and wisdom is often elusive. But it doesn't have to be that way; in middle age we can change our patterns of behavior, and recalculate our priorities so that when we do reach our golden years the reflection we experience will be fulfilling and genuine. The last thing we want at this stage of life is to feel useless and unappreciated.

Many of us know older people who seem miserable and lacking in compassion. One may argue that has to do with their status, the monetary considerations, as well as health. That strikes more of an excuse than a reason. It has more to do with how they prepared for the reflective years of their lives. My Mother was in terrible health the final few years of her life; she had to take all kinds of medication each and every day and visit doctors on a more than regular basis. She had lung cancer, coronary artery disease, terrible arthritis, and the list goes on. She lived in a senior citizen high rise in what was called a studio apartment. Her income was fixed and limited even after working her entire adult life. My Mother was even a World War II veteran; something I was always quite proud of. Even with all that seemed to have gone against her, she still managed to find joy in living. It would take her the entire day to get on the bus and go grocery shopping, but she did it without complaint. She never asked for help in doing something she believed she was perfectly capable of doing herself, even if it took her hours to accomplish. Even as I reached my early forties, my Mother continued to worry about me, and all of those things mothers do for their children. People were her joy and her responsibility. Money meant next to nothing to her; she spent it when she got it. More often than not, she would spend it on others before herself. She never even wanted cable TV. All she needed was a good book and the phone to speak with her grandchildren.

My Mother followed both paths in life simultaneously: the internal and the external. No one told her to, that was just who she was. I suspect that's where I learned the value of continued nurturing of the inner self as I was growing up. She didn't teach it; she lived it. I remember quite vividly coming home from work when her hips hurt so bad she could hardly walk and seeing her down to the field by my house playing softball with my kids. They loved her; we all loved her for who she was, not what she had. Her attitudes transcended many popular ideas when she was growing up. I never heard my Mother say a derogatory thing about anyone, race, creed, religion, or ethnic group. In fact, I had absolutely no idea what prejudice was until I started going to school and heard about it from others. To this day I still can't understand bigotry, prejudice, the perceived logic behind negative ideas when it comes to other human beings. Again, my Mother didn't teach that; she lived it. I remember something my Mother said not too long before she died. We were all in the hospital with my daughter when someone said something to my Mom about it was too bad she couldn't afford to take a cab up. The conversation drifted into what people had, what they didn't have, and what they wanted. My Mother offered to the conversation that she had everything she needed in life, and always did. Someone looked at her a bit askew, and said, "Oh really." My Mother just smiled her impish little grin and returned, "Oh yes, I have my memories." She left the conversation with that, and she was right and she was triumphant.

We can find that serenity in life anytime we want to open ourselves up to it; we don't have to wait until we retire when we are programmed to relax and reflect. That inner peace of mind, sense of spiritual fulfillment can be realized at any stage of life. As middle agers we have the opportunity to find that wisdom and peace. We have followed the path of acquiring knowledge; we have and continue to follow the path of acquiring experience. All we need to do is to make the conscience choice to follow both paths at the same time. Experience can be much more fulfilling when we are at peace with who we are and what our place is here on this earth. A book that deals so well with these issues is *Siddhartha*, by Herman Hesse. It deals with the three stages of life, but strictly from the internal point of view. What Hesse suggests is that life should be lived from the inside out, not the other way around. Now is the time to stop allowing external reality, something we have little control over, to shape your inner vision of yourself. Find out who you are and be in charge of your own reality. Allow your heart and mind to guide you, not your senses. Your senses are fickle and only want immediate gratification. Joy lasts for ever.

CHAPTER 10

EXPECTATIONS

When we were younger we probably expected quite a bit from life; I know I did. Sometimes we realized our hopes and dreams and sometimes we didn't. If life was simple we would all be exactly where we wanted to be right now, but it isn't. We make choices, and plans, and do the best we can to try and reach our goals. But guess what, not everyone we encounter in life has the same goals as we do, or even respects our goals. Hell, everyone else has his own agenda as well. Most of us, as we reflect in middle age, most likely reached some if not all of the big goals we set for ourselves. I had a house once; a whole bunch of different cars, even a sports car once; a family, and a decent job to boot. Some of us still have those things we set out to acquire, some of us don't. It doesn't really matter in the long run, because what is truly important is still attainable. I know I didn't realize what was really important until I started to pay attention to the small decisions I made as intently as the big ones. It is often the little, even daily decisions that we make that can most profoundly affect each moment of our lives.

Most of us spend a considerable amount of time planning to go to school, buy a house, get married, buy a car, get cable TV, the internet and all kinds of other things that are important to our lives. There's even plenty of help available for most of these big decisions about life. There are all kinds of well intentioned people out there who would be more than happy to give us all kinds of advice based on their efforts and experience. But that's them, not you. People, even people who love you, can give you all kinds of what seems to be great advice, but when all is said and done, you are the only one who has to live with your decisions; you and your family. Count on yourself. No one, absolutely no one, has ever duplicated a life and the experiences that go along with that life. Let's not lose sight of the fact that we are all individuals. In the entire history of the world there has never been, nor ever will be, someone else like you; you are unique; one of a kind. Always remember that when faced with a decision and you have advice coming at you from every direction.

Make the little decisions count each and every day. Do the best you can and learn to live with the decisions you make, and when you happen to make the wrong decisions, do all you can to make things right again. One can never end a marriage in the right way; there is no right way to break up a family. I regret deeply how I handled the same situation when it happened to me, but I can't turn the clock back. I wish I could, but we all know that is not within our power. So I have to move on and try to make up for the bad decisions that I made way back when. I think, hope, and pray I have tried as best I can to make up for some of the lousy decisions I am guilty of, but only the people who were hurt by what happened can judge that. I have tried to make amends with time and money and understanding; and I continue to do all I can. I will never stop because a family will always be there. No matter how old the children get, or how far apart their mother and I grow, the fact remains that we will always have that connection. There comes a time when it is necessary to put regret and guilt behind and move on in a positive direction.

The choices we make when it comes to emotional issues are often emotionally based; that just stands to reason. So when we make choices based on emotion, we are guided by emotion, and emotion can be a faulty guide. I could never effectively argue with anyone with whom I had an emotional attachment, still can't. I lose every time, and more often than not end up making a fool out of myself. I now accept that about myself and try to avoid confrontations that get the better of me emotionally. Instead I try and think things out ahead of time and prepare for the confrontation in order to deal with the issues in an intelligent and well thought out way. Don't make the decision in a flash to get angry. Put off the anger until you are calm and can think. Again, pay attention to the small decisions you make every day of your life, and you may find that you are making better choices that can only serve you and the people you love better.

Think about some of the seemingly minor choices you were faced with in the past, and consider where those choices have led you. I remember when I met the woman who would become the Mother of my children. It was Christmas Eve, 1969. I was 17 years old and she was 14. My friend Larry and I had been at his brother's house having a few beers when we decided to go to Midnight Mass. We arrived just on time, and like all of the cool kids in the late 60's we stood in the back of the church for the service. We left right before the end and stood out at the bottom of the side door steps just hanging out and smoking, being as cool as we could be in the midnight winter air. As the church was emptying, I noticed a beautiful young girl standing all alone by the church door. I couldn't take my eyes off of her. She had dark hair, a beautiful face, and a petite figure. I pointed her out to Larry, and he agreed she was fine.

Throughout my adolescence, I had never been what one would call today a Player. I was generally shy with girls and rarely asked anyone out. I found it easier to just hang out with my friends and avoid rejection. So I usually admired girls from afar. That night would be different. It seemed like a small thing to do, approach a girl, but for me it took a bit of courage. I walked up the steps and said hello. She returned the greeting. It turned out that she knew who I was because she had often seen me on the street corner with my friends when she would drive by with her parents. I even wrote a poem about that many years later. In fact I wrote a lot of poems about those early years and the struggles we all have at that age. But I didn't know who she was; had never seen her before. We lived in basically the same neighborhood, but went to different schools. What came out of my mouth next was totally unplanned. I asked her if I could walk her home. I never even considered what a ridiculous question that was to ask a stranger; but I asked it anyway.

She smiled and I noticed how small she seemed. Her smile seemed to glow and made me feel warm. She told me she was waiting for some friends to come out of church. My next line has to go down in whatever records are kept for such follies as one of the worst pick up lines ever. I told her, well if they don't show up can I walk you home? Like they were lost in the bowels of the church and would never be heard from again. Why wouldn't they show up? Of course that thought never entered my mind. I said okay and rejoined my friend at the bottom of the steps to wait and see if her friends would show up.

Larry was getting cold by this point and tried to talk me into leaving. I wasn't cold at all and almost started walking away with him. She continued to wait by the door and didn't seem to be in any hurry to walk off with me. So Larry and I started to walk away, but after a few steps I turned around. She was still there. I don't really think I gave it much thought at all when I told Larry to go ahead and I walked back to the church. I walked up the steps, stood in front of her and said, "Come on, let's go." To my surprise she started walking with me. I asked her about her friends and she told me they knew their way home. We exchanged the basic information on the way to her house; names, ages, schools. I asked her if I could call her and she said it was okay, her number was in the book. When we got to her house, I didn't try and kiss her or anything like that; I didn't know her. We just said Merry Christmas and good-bye.

When I arrived home that night it must have been after 2 a.m. My Mother was still up sitting at the kitchen table reading as she often did late at night or early in the morning. All of the presents were neatly wrapped under the tree. Even at 17 Christmas was usually an exciting time for me; I couldn't wait to see what I had received as gifts. But this night seemed so different. All I wanted to do was sit in the kitchen and talk to my Mother. She knew something was up and asked me what was going on, I seemed preoccupied. The first thing I said to her was that I met the girl I was going to marry. My Mother never tired of telling that story. But it was the truth. I don't know how I knew it, I just did. And we did get married, and have three beautiful children, and eventually broke up. But if not for that minor, unplanned decision to leave Larry and walk back to the church, my life would have turned out totally differently than it did. It was seemingly that small decision that had the profoundest of effects on me. Our lives are full of those kind of choices; the choices that really matter and count for the most. In order for me to fully understand where I am today, I need to take a look at where I have been to make sense out of my life and try and come to terms with what has shaped me and my attitudes about everything.

FORGIVENESS

Sometimes it is difficult to move on to a better place when we are holding on so tight to something from our past, something that won't leave us alone. Finding and discovering renewal, a new light to guide us through a reawakening can be sabotaged by our own feelings and guilt and regrets at what we might have done in the past, or what we might have failed to do in the past. But living with the past is living in a dead past;

therefore living a dead life. No matter what the past may have been all about, there is nothing we can do about it now. No one, as far as I know, has the power to turn the clock back and right a wrong or make a different choice.

It's important to accept our humanness, because if we don't, no one else will. Before anyone else can find forgiveness for you, you have to first be willing to forgive yourself. Often we are the most difficult to forgive, because we know the truth, and are sometimes afraid to admit the truth. Unless you've lived in a monastery or closet, middle age usually has been gained with some living, good and bad. We all make bad choices in our lives; do bad things to ourselves and other people. Now is the time to admit those things to yourself and forgive yourself for being human. If it helps, seek the forgiveness of others who you may have wronged. But don't always plan on others' forgiveness. Not everyone may be prepared to forgive. Forgetting is something totally different; no one can forget, but everyone has it in his power to forgive. Forgiving yourself is the first step.

I, like many middleagers, have many things I wish I could change about my past, but know that I can't; I can only go on and try to be a better person in the future. I regret not being a better son to my Mother. I remember the last time I saw her before she died. I was dropping her off at home after a lengthy visit to my daughter in the hospital. I was other directed, as one might imagine, and not terribly concerned about her feelings. I mentioned something about not being able to give her rides home after the hospital every night; she needed to seek alternatives. She agreed, understanding my request; and I flippantly told her good-bye. That was the last time I saw her alive. Sure, I didn't know she would die within a day or two, but the fact remains I was unconcerned with her feelings. See, I knew she would and has forgiven me, but I couldn't forgive myself at first. I felt terribly guilty and didn't even mention it to anyone. We tend to hide our guilt for fear of being judged negatively. It took me a year, but I was eventually able to forgive myself and find solace in the good memories, as we all do. But we can only truly find comfort in the memories of our lives when forgiveness is a gift that we give to ourselves.

I couldn't even begin to list everything I believe I was and am responsible for during my marriage and the break up of my family. When a marriage ends, a family is torn apart no matter how much we want to deny that part of it. You see, true forgiveness can only come when we are honest with ourselves. Only with the truth can we find relief, and the opportunity to move on to make sense of our lives and be who we need to be for ourselves and others. Tell yourself the truth, and accept the truth. I wasn't what one would call a good husband; I was a pretty good father, but not a husband. Sure, the kids' Mother had something to do with the end of the marriage, but those things are her issues, not mine. Everyone has his or her own story to tell, and we all know that the truth lies somewhere in the middle. I can only admit my faults and the mistakes that I made. These are the issues I need to admit to myself, and forgive myself for my actions. Only with the truth and forgiveness can I hope to move on and avoid the same mistakes in the future. Tell yourself the truth, write it down, accept that you are human, and forgive yourself. You are an important, and as I have said before, a unique, one of a kind individual. You have a lot of love and compassion to offer to the people you come into contact with everyday; but you need to offer yourself that love and compassion first. You get from life what you give to it.

There are many different ways we can address this Karma thing; what goes around comes around stuff. But there is truth in the obvious. If you spend your days being an asshole to people, treating them bad, then that's probably what you'll get back from them and the world. You might not get it immediately, but you will experience what you have been responsible for others experiencing. It's just a matter of attitude, not being happy; that's why people are not nice to people; they feel bad themselves, so they try and get others to sail in their flimsy boats. It's all about energy and attitude.

Think about it a minute. Let's say you go into work in a really bad mood because your team lost the big game, or your wife wasn't in the mood because you were a jerk all weekend, but you're all upset because she should just understand you and constantly forgive you for having no consideration for her, so you're pissed. Everyone at work knows you're someplace they don't want to go, so they avoid you and your wonderful company. Wake up; you're doing it to yourself. If you hate the world, it will avoid you; if you love the world and life, the world and life will give that back to you. It may as simple as you feeling better about yourself and each and every day you live. We only get a finite number of days, so why live them like an asshole? Live your numbered days like each and every one of them will be your last. Live a lifetime in each and every day.

It's not hard to live a lifetime in each and every day. It's just a matter of trying your best to experience all of the emotions God has given you as a gift. Laugh with your children, cry with your wife, remember those who are no longer here and be grateful you knew them. Remember, death doesn't end a relationship; our limited conception of reality and the unlimited potential beyond reality keeps us from being open minded. Open your mind and let life - the past, the moment, and the future - in; let it all in at one time, travel all paths at the same time and get rid of the regrets and stop making mistakes. Make that your goal: living a lifetime each and every day of your life. Remember the most important thing you can do is to love, and that love will be returned to you. If it isn't always, the power of your love will always sustain you. Don't be afraid of experiencing emotions. Let your heart grow along with your body, mind, and spirit.

ATTITUDES

Changing your attitudes about many things can go a long way in finding renewal and growth. Sure you have discovered and maybe even believe you need to forgive yourself, but you also need to understand that forgiving others is also a big part of change. It's kind of like that twelve step program a lot of self help groups employ. It's all about a process that leads to renewal and a renaissance of the body, mind, and spirit. Holding grudges only wears on you, not the person you're mad at. Let it go, and free yourself for the rest of your life. Look at your attitudes and see which ones need to be changed. What human values have you given thought to recently? Have you thought about love, dignity, self-esteem, freedom, attitudes toward woman for example?

Of all of the things one can possibly have in life, love has to be right up at the top of the list. But it isn't only about being loved; it's also about loving, and caring for others who are important to you. But it can extend beyond that as well. There are all kinds of different love we can offer to the world: you can love your friends in one way, and your neighbors in another. Part of this love stuff is also about forgiveness, too. Having love in your heart also opens up the possibilities for more choices in life. Having choices should be right up there with love. We are all born with the potential for good or evil. We can choose to be good, not only to ourselves but also to the people we come in contact with every day. We have that choice. We can choose to be in a good mood; we can choose not to worry when worrying won't do any good except take up brain time. We can choose to do the right thing, and choose to accept failure and learn from it. Give yourself the gift of love and choices; you are the only one who can control your heart. Eric Fromm expands on these points in his book, *The Art of Loving.*

Dignity is also something we can give to ourselves. It's all about making the right choices and feeling comfortable with who you are. When my children were younger, I always insisted they treat people with respect. I taught them to respect everyone they meet until they lose your respect through their actions. Always start out regarding people in a positive way. Say thank you, please, listen when someone talks to you; give everyone you can the gift of your time. My kids went through all of the rebellious stages most kids go through. They had their moments, more than their share of being disrespectful to their mother and me, but they were always respectful toward others. My children present themselves with dignity, and they are received with dignity. Dignity is also about trying not to make decisions that you might regret or feel ashamed of. That isn't always possible, of course, but it is worth the effort. If shame does find its way into your heart, treat it as a lesson and avoid it in the future. Aristotle believed we could not have civilization without embarrassment. Being dignified means acting appropriately in any social situation, no matter what level of society you may find yourself involved with. What that means is people on the street deserve your respect just as much as those who seem to demand respect simply because of money or social status.

Learn to love yourself if you don't already, and allow your self-esteem to show through. Avoid arrogance and practice developing an attitude that is based on knowing who you are, not who you want people to think you are. Life seems to be a race, and it's not a race to see who can die with the most stuff. It's a race to see who can leave this earth having left it a better place. If you truly like yourself, your self-esteem is in tact, you will be remembered for you, not your nice car. Don't worry about what others think of you if you live your life positively. Anyone who questions your value is dealing with an issue of theirs, not yours. Don't allow others to chop away at your self-esteem; it is up to you to determine who you are and what your value is. I had a problem with self-esteem when I was growing up. I think we all go through that at one time or another. I thought I had less value then my friends because they all lived in houses and had fathers and cars and yards and a dog to chase, or be chased by. I see now I didn't have to feel that way; that's the beauty of a middle age renaissance. You can even change your past and turn it into something that was positive. We all do the best we can, even our parents. Give them and you a break. Treasure your past; it is what in part made you who you are today. We are all memory; make that memory and yourself swell with self-esteem. Sorry, now I'm starting to get a bit cheesy. Wouldn't you agree? Like yourself and bathe as often as possible.

With self-esteem, you will also find that being an individual opens up new possibilities for your future, and helps you make sense of your past. Throughout our lives we are encouraged to follow some sort of leader. Whether it's the cool kid at school, or the family in the neighborhood who seem to have the most stuff, we want to be somebody else. There is absolutely nothing wrong with being who we are; the new person we are striving to become each and every day of our lives. There is no template for being a man, in spite of what mass media might have you believe. It is okay to display emotion; it is okay to be affectionate with your wife or significant other, even in public. If someone judges you for not acting the macho, quintessential male, that is his problem, not yours. He is not going to kiss you goodnight, bathe your children, worry about your health, hold you when you're sad, or be there at the end. Give yourself to your woman, and make her happy, love her, cherish her for all she is and all you both can be. Decide what really matters in life right now, and make those things your priorities from now on. Remember, we all love in different ways, and no one can be somebody else. Stop expecting people, especially those who love you, to be you; let them be who they are and nurture who they are, and cherish who they are as they most certainly will you.

BEGINNING
I am constantly involved in the process of making myself a better person. It's not a burden; it's a joyful challenge to

become someone new, someone better, and someone who can find love, happiness and fulfillment for the rest of his life. Recently I was discussing my health with my doctor, among other things, and he asked me when I began my regime of physical, mental, and spiritual renewal. I told him that I was about 39 when it all began for me in earnest. His response was, then I guess it's not too late for me. I don't know how old he is, but it doesn't matter. It is never too late to begin all over again and make it right. Hell, now you have the wisdom, experience and strength to be truly successful at becoming who you were meant to be all along. It's all here. I did it and continue to do it. All you have to do is to give yourself the gift of change, and the joy of choice; the right choices. So forget the fact that you are middle aged and move into the second half, the better half of your life. Only you can make the decision to do it. But once you do make the decision, your life and everyone's life that you touch will benefit from your journey of renewal. Body, Mind, and Spirit all work together. It's time we all began to recognize that fact. It's time to build your body for health and self-esteem; to build your mind for wisdom and truth; to build your spirit for love and joy. Good Luck; have faith in yourself. Open your eyes and look around; take a break from the texting, tweeting, internet surfing and whatever else takes you away from the real world around you. Limit the virtual reality and embrace the real world of the senses and the heart.

APPENDIX A

SUGGESTIONS FOR THE GYM

Choosing a workout routine is generally pretty basic. You have to find one that works best for you, your body type, and your initial level of strength and endurance. Don't take chances when beginning; always start with light weight until you can determine what you can handle. Move the weight up slowly.

Lifting weights in a gym is all about sets and repetitions. A set consists of repetitions manipulating the weight or machine. For example, if you were doing bicep curls you might choose 20-pound weights and curl those ten times. Each curl is a repetition, or rep, and the full ten is a set. For maximum benefit you need to do a minimum of three sets per exercise.

FREE WEIGHTS

Free weights are made up of dumbbells and barbells. Dumbbells are the individually hand held weights. They can range from two pounds up to over 200 pounds each. The 200 pound dumbbells are for the scary guys in the gyms we don't go to. Barbells are the long bars holding individual plates. The plates range in weight from 2 1/2 pounds up to

45 pounds each. The primary benefit of using free weights is they not only work the primary muscle you are targeting but also the stabilizer muscle associated with the primary muscle. The majority of injuries that occur in gyms are generally associated with the use of free weights.

People hurt themselves with free weights because they are not using their heads when they are working their muscles. Some people over estimate their strength and pile on more than they can handle. I can't remember the number of times I or someone else had to lift a barbell off the chest of an individual over estimating his strength. Luckily, the times I or someone I observed assisted, no one was seriously injured. But why take the chance? If you choose to use free weights, begin light and work your way up slowly. As much as we might hate to admit it, we are not 20 years old or 30 or 40, and some of us aren't 50.

It wasn't terribly long ago, maybe two or three years, I was bench pressing (laying flat on a bench working the chest) 80 pound dumbbells. Now the muscles may be willing, but the joints aren't. I have had to adjust. I still use dumbbells, but lighter ones. I now compensate by doing more exercises on machines.

WEIGHT MACHINES

There are all kinds of machines available in gyms today. They are individually designed to work a specific muscle or muscle group. There are machines for practically every muscle in the body below the neck. With some, you change the weight by moving a key up and down a stack of weights. Others are designed where you actually can use the barbell plates without the potential danger. It is generally safer to test your limits on weight machines, but still not advisable. You don't want to pull, wrench or otherwise injure a muscle. Muscle injury recovery can often take quite a while. I once tore a pectoral (chest) muscle and it took weeks to heal. I didn't stop working out, I just compensated for the healing period. This is where learning to read your body is helpful. I suspect most of us over 40 will opt for the machines more than the free weights. Just remember, weight is weight and it all works the same.

To learn more about these options pick up one of the popular muscle magazines on the market. This is a good way to begin to familiarize yourself with what's available. Also, when you finally choose a gym most will offer an initial tour of their facilities and offer explanations as to how to use the equipment. When all else fails, or isn't quite enough, most machines actually come with little direction cards on them. And as we already know, paying attention to someone who looks like he knows what he's doing is a good way to figure out the equipment.

BREAKING IT DOWN

It is difficult to get a complete body workout by going to the gym only a day or two a week. Commit a minimum of three days to a maximum of six days. Each day should be devoted to a body part, or symmetrical group of muscles. For example, when working your back also work your biceps on that day. You see, when working your back muscles you are also indirectly working your biceps. Or when working your pecs also work your triceps. The movements require to work these muscles compliment each other.

Even before I joined a gym I would get home from work and go directly to my bedroom to exercise. All I had was one set of 20 pound dumbbells. Even then I knew that I had to allow at least 24 hours to elapse between working out the same muscle. You see, a muscle is broken down when tested with weight. It needs time to recover and grow to compensate for the weight resistance. If you work the same muscle every day, you don't give it time to recover, only time to continue to breakdown.

PRE-GYM WORKOUT

Monday – 3 sets of pushups – 25 reps for each set.
    Sit-ups – 2 sets of 30 reps.
    Tricep kick backs – 3 sets of 20 reps.

Tuesday – 3 sets of bicep curls (20 lb. dumbbells) – 20 reps.
3 sets of shoulder presses – 15 reps.

Wednesday – 3 sets leg squats (holding 20 lb. dumbbells) – 15 reps.
Sit-ups – 2 sets of 30 reps.

Thursday – repeat Monday's routine.

Friday – repeat Tuesday,s routine.

Weekends off.

I followed this basic routine for a number of years prior to joining a gym. I of course would vary it occasionally just to keep it fresh and as interesting as exercise can be. I wasn't building a lot of muscle but I was keeping in shape. I also bicycled for my cardiovascular workout. I still ride a bike today, but it's a stationary bike in the gym.

Once I did join a gym I began with comparatively light weights. Also, don't forget to watch others to learn.

BASIC WORKOUT

A basic and beneficial workout can be accomplished in a minimum of three days a week at the gym. It can be three days in a row, or skip a day in between.

Monday – Chest – 8 to 12 sets of machine or free weight presses. The number of reps should be no fewer than five or more than 15. If you can do 15 the weight is probably on the light side. This can include the incline and the decline movement – mix it up. Triceps – 4 to 8 sets of tricep movements. Lots of options to check out here. Do 2 or 3 sets of stomach crunches too. In fact, do stomach crunches every day if you can work it in. The stomach, forearm and calve muscles are muscles that we use every day; therefore we can work them every day if so inclined. Also do some cardio if you can work it in.

Tuesday – Back – 8 to 12 sets of machine movements. Do 8 to 12 reps where you can really feel the last one – it's a bit of a challenge. Remember to read your body and keep it safe. Biceps – 8 to 12 sets of machine and/or free weight curl movements. Here do up to 15 reps where the final few are again a bit of a challenge. Don't forget the crunches and cardio.
Wednesday – Legs – 8 to 12 sets of machine movements. Do up to 15 reps., and don't forget the challenge. Calves – 5 to 10 sets on appropriate calve equipment. Up to 30 reps per set. My calves are my weakest body part, so I'm always doing a little extra here.

Shoulders – 8 to 12 sets of machine and/or free weight presses/3 to 5 sets of lateral raises/3 to 5 sets of shrugs. And yes, crunches and cardio too.

This same workout can be repeated twice a week by taking a day off in between. So, you would do the three day workout, take a day off, and repeat. This would allow for adequate recovery time, and maximum strength and muscle building benefits.

INTERMEDIATE

Once you're in the swing and your workouts have pretty much become habit, you should begin to feel a difference in three weeks. And as you progress, you should actually begin to see a difference in your physique in six weeks or less. The primary way to step up your routine is simply by adding additional weight to what you already are doing in the gym. It is best to add weight slowly, say about five pounds at a time with free weights, and no more than ten pound increments at a time with machine weights. Keep a notebook if it will help you to keep track of what you're lifting. It will also provide you with a daily log to show progress and track success.

ADVANCED

Once you've been at it a while, you might discover your routine is becoming boring, or you've plateaued and aren't building muscle as quickly as when you began. This is natural; your body has adjusted to the resistance and has compensated by building the muscle necessary to meet the challenge. Time for a change. Mix it up. Change the days you have been working specific body parts; go from free weights to machines, and visa versa. And now that you've been at it for months, it is also time to add a bit more weight. But be sure to do it safely. Add only that which you can manipulate at least six to eight times. Advanced simply means that you've been at it a year or more. Give yourself a pat on the back, and shake it up for year number two.

APPENDIX B

SUGGESTED READING LIST

Like the saying goes, "The mind is a terrible thing to waste." What's the point of having a great, okay, good body if the mind doesn't compliment it? As discussed previously, many of us have lost touch with our intellectual selves with our busy lives, and pursuit of our dreams. Most of what most of us read by the time we hit middle age is probably just providing us with information; it's not stimulating the intellect. What follows is a suggested reading list to kick start the brain in realizing its full potential. The list is eclectic. It's a beginning.

BOOKS
Johnny Got His Gun by Dalton Trumbo.
This book is about many things, but it's primarily about the power of the human spirit, and the value of life.

Moby Dick by Herman Melville.
A timeless classic about good vs. evil, man vs. nature, and which is which.

Typee by Herman Melville.
One of the books that made the author famous during his lifetime. It's a great and challenging story to read.

Siddhartha by Herman Hesse.
A wonderful story combing Western and Eastern philosophies dealing with the essence of what we are and what we desire, and what is truly important.

The Things They Carried by Tim O'Brien.
The context is the Vietnam War, but the reality of the book is about choices we all make, and the good and bad things we do for love.

One Flew Over the Cuckoo's Nest by Ken Kesey.
A great story about perception, rebellion, and conformity. There are many layers to this story; treasures to be discovered by reading carefully.

A Handmaid's Tale by Margaret Atwood.
A compelling story about class, human value, and the roles men and women play in society. Although the story suggests it takes place in the future, the careful reader can figure out what the author is saying about society in the past and present.

Lord of the Flies by William Goldman.
The book is about a group of young men stranded on a deserted island and how the situation encourages them to rely on their basic animal instincts. It's really about our society and the choices we make in order to fit in and survive.

The Bluest Eye by Toni Morrison.
A wonderful story about wanting to be more than we are, and discovering that who we are is a good thing. (Actually I would recommend anything by Toni Morrison.)

Catch 22 by Joseph Heller..
A wonderfully challenging book about the absurdity of war, and how that absurdity reflects upon life.

Catcher in the Rye by J.D. Salinger.
A classic about youth, rebellion and the questions that matter to all people, like, what's the point?

The Road by Cormac McCarthy
A Messianic parable of the highest order about the beauty and simplicity of what love and relationships are about.

The preceding list is a beginning. All of the works suggested are what is considered modern literature. Certainly the timeless classics are something you should explore once you're back on the reading track. Libraries are a great place to begin and continue upon this journey. These books certainly reflect my tastes, but they are each and every one worth the time and the effort. Even E-books are an option — but my books are made out of paper. At the conclusion of an Introduction to Literature class one semester, I had a young man come up to and shake my hand, thanking me. He said, "I am so glad I took this class; I didn't know what I was missing." Don't miss out: READ.

POETS
Poetry, more than anything else, helps us to understand the triumphs and tragedies of life. What follows is a suggested list of poets.

Maya Angelou	Robert Frost
Galway Kinnell	Sylvia Plath
Yusef Komunyakaa	Robert Pinsky
Rita Dove	Richard Wilbur
Lucille Clifton	Stanley Kunitz

Seamus Heaney   Etheridge Knight
Carl Sandburg   Gwendolyn Brooks
Walt Whitman   Bob Dylan
and Woody Guthrie

Like the list of books, this is a suggested reading list; a place to begin your journey of growth, renewal, your renaissance.